50 YARDS OF FUN

KNITTING TOYS from SCRAP YARN

Martingale®
Create with Confidence

50 Yards of Fun: Knitting Toys from Scrap Yarn
© 2013 by Rebecca Danger

Martingale®
19021 120th Ave. NE, Ste. 102
Bothell, WA 98011-9511 USA
ShopMartingale.com

Printed in China
18 17 16 15 14 13   8 7 6 5 4 3 2 1

Library of Congress Cataloging-in-Publication Data is available upon request.

ISBN: 978-1-60468-303-5

Mission Statement

Dedicated to providing quality products and service to inspire creativity.

CREDITS

President and CEO: Tom Wierzbicki

Editor in Chief: Mary V. Green

Design Director: Paula Schlosser

Managing Editor: Karen Costello Soltys

Acquisitions Editor: Karen M. Burns

Technical Editor: Ursula Reikes

Copy Editor: Tiffany Mottet

Production Manager: Regina Girard

Cover and Interior Designer: Adrienne Smitke

Photographer: Brent Kane

Illustrator: Adrienne Smitke

Dedication

This book is dedicated to knitters everywhere. Thanks for being such a supportive, creative, and all-around amazing group of folks.

Contents

Introduction

Hello and welcome to *50 Yards of Fun!* I am so excited you're here, because I have a fun pile of patterns for you in the following pages. My pattern writing adventure that started back in early 2009 really began with my first free pattern, Bunny Nuggets (shown below). I designed Bunny Nuggets to be a quick, easy, perfect way to use up all of those leftover bits of yarn we knitters always seem to have. Over the last several years, after two more equally popular tiny knitting patterns and several thousand Bunny Nugget projects popping up on Ravelry.com, I decided it was time for me to do a whole book's worth of tiny knitting projects.

I love the idea of having quick little projects to use up your scrap yarn or handspun yarns with short yardage. I love them for beginner and kid knitters, for unique little gifts, as decorations for holidays or as party favors. I love them because, with just a little bit of creativity, an experienced knitter can turn one little project into a plethora of variations. In short, I love tiny knitted projects for a million reasons and I know you will too. They are kind of like potato chips: I bet you won't be able to knit just one!

In these pages, you'll find a wonderful selection of patterns. With everything from a cute, more traditional Dinky Doggy (page 65) to a bit more unusual Little Luchador (page 48), I know that this book has something for everyone. I hope this serves as an abundant source of patterns for all of you beginner knitters, or a jumping-off point for all of you experienced knitters to take and run with and create your own variations.

Wishing you many happy knitting adventures,

~ Rebecca

The pattern that started it all, Bunny Nuggets, is available as a free download on my blog, RebeccaDanger.typepad.com.

How This Book Works

This book has patterns for five body shapes, then expands on those shapes to create a variety of different projects.

I designed all of the patterns to take about 50 yards of worsted-weight yarn (although a few took a little bit more). All of my samples were knit using worsted-weight yarn on US size 5 needles to give you a general idea of size and yardage. You can make any project smaller or larger by using thinner or thicker yarn and appropriate-size needles. If you're using yarn that is thicker than worsted weight, you'll probably need a bit more yardage. For thinner yarn, you'll probably need slightly less yardage. Just for fun, I knit the Basic Peanut-Body in six different yarn weights (listed below) so you can see the variation you'll get using different-sized yarns and needles.

You'll find several projects for each body shape, but believe me, it was hard to narrow this book down to just those projects. I had so many ideas, and I know you will too! Since all of the bodies are similarly sized, you can easily use an arm, ear, or nose from one shape with a different-shaped body to get a whole new critter. Have fun and let those creative juices start flowing.

YARN WEIGHT		NEEDLES	APPROX YARDAGE	EYE SIZE	APPROX HEIGHT (from head to toe)
1	Heritage Sock from Cascade Yarns	US size 1 (2.25 mm)	5 g (22 yds)	9 mm	3½"
2	Heritage 150 Sock Yarn from Cascade Yarns	US size 2 (2.75 mm)	6 g (20 yds)	9 mm	4"
3	220 Superwash Sport from Cascade Yarns	US size 4 (3.5 mm)	10 g (28 yds)	12 mm	5"
4	220 Superwash from Cascade Yarns	US size 5 (3.75 mm)	14 g (31 yds)	12 mm	5½"
5	128 Superwash from Cascade Yarns	US size 7 (4.5 mm)	29 g (38 yds)	15 mm	7½"
6	Magnum from Cascade Yarns	US size 11 (8 mm)	132 g (65 yds)	15 mm	13"

Little Knits Guidelines

Here you'll find some basic information on what you need to make the critters in this book. Though I wrote *50 Yards of Fun* assuming you have basic knitting knowledge, I know there are a few techniques that would be easier with a bit of explanation. For additional techniques, see "Where to Go for Help" on page 14.

LITTLE GAUGES

I didn't call for a specific gauge for any of the projects in this book. All the patterns are written round by round so that you can pick whatever size yarn and needles you want to use. Simply use smaller needles than those recommended on the yarn label to create a tighter knitted fabric so the stuffing doesn't show through. My rule of thumb is to go down two or three needle sizes from the smallest recommended needle size for your yarn. For example, I knit my Cascade 220 from Cascade Yarns on US size 5 (3.75 mm) needles instead of the recommended US size 7 (4.5 mm) or 8 (5 mm) needles. Depending on your personal knitting style, this may be right on for you, or you may want to go up or down a size. Play around to figure out what works best for you.

Because you can pick your yarn and needle size, you can make all sorts of sizes of critters from each of these patterns. Check out my cool size comparison (page 7) for a general idea of how each body can be made smaller or larger depending on your needles and yarn. Think of how far you can take these patterns just by using different yarn and needles. Mind boggling, isn't it?

Remember, larger yarn and needles mean larger critters, smaller yarn and needles mean smaller critters. Got it? Good. Now get knitting!

LITTLE YARDAGES

Since this book is called *50 Yards of Fun,* I kept close track of how much yarn I was using for each project. I have included the approximate worsted-weight yardage I used to give you an idea of how much yardage you'll need. My intention was to help you pick which projects you have enough yardage for, or if you want to make a certain project but feel you might be short on yarn, to help you modify the pattern to make it work for you. For instance, if you have less yardage than what's called for, you can decide to shorten arms, or take out wings or ears, or add stripes or what-have-you. Take a peek at the pattern's required yardage before you dive into a project you don't have enough yarn for!

I like to determine my yardage by weighing my yarn. I use a regular kitchen scale I picked up for under $20 and I always weigh my yarn using grams. To figure out how much yardage is in your weight, look at the weight versus yards numbers on your yarn label. If your label says 100 grams and 220 yards, you can figure that 220 yards divided by 100 grams means you'll have 2.2 yards per gram. Pretty nifty, huh? So for a worsted-weight yarn of 100 grams and 220 yards, you can expect to get approximately 50 yards in 23 grams. I find this is the easiest way to determine yardage, but some folks feel it's not 100% accurate. You can also purchase a yardage counter to be more precise.

BASIC TOOL KIT FOR ALL PATTERNS

Since most of these patterns will need the same notions, I've listed them all in one place to save you the repetition. Your basic tool kit should include:

⌘ Approximately 50 yards (23 grams) of worsted-weight yarn

⌘ 40"-long circular needle, 2 or 3 sizes smaller than what is recommended for your yarn (for Magic Loop method), or a set of 4 or 5 double-pointed needles

⌘ Notions: scissors, tapestry needle, safety eyes/noses, scrap yarn for embroidering face, stuffing, stitch markers, row counter (optional)

If you need anything not on this list, it will be included on the pattern page.

PICKING YARNS FOR LITTLE KNITS

Oh yarn, how I love you. I designed these little knits to use up all of those little bits of leftover yarns from bigger projects, or even from yarns in your stash. Seriously, anything goes for these projects. Lace yarn to super bulky, acrylic to alpaca, it doesn't matter; they will all make awesome little knits. Whatever type of yarn floats your knitted boat, go for it. I even found eyelash yarn, of which I am not a fan, awesomely awesome for these projects. (Check out my Yea-Big Yeti below and on page 66; he's one of my favorites!) If you're knitting with more than one type of yarn for a single project, be sure to match the weight of the yarns as much as possible for the most uniform finished item.

I am always here to encourage you to buy more yarn. With this book in your hands, full of tiny knits that a ball of yarn will always provide more than enough yardage for, feel the power to walk through any yarn store and buy with gay abandon! I mean it. Buying yarn is not only good for the economy; it's good for your soul. If someone gives you a hard time about it you can say, "But Rebecca Danger told me to buy more yarn because I have *50 Yards of Fun,* which means I will always have something to do with any yarn I buy!" And when he or she doesn't believe you, you pull out this book and show off this paragraph.

As I was writing this book, I did happen to stumble across a few cool little yarn items I wanted to share with you. It seems like many yarn companies are starting to sell short-yardage skeins. I know there are several indie dyers that even have short-yardage clubs these days. I think the

cool Lion Brand Bonbons pack and the nifty bundle of sock yarn mini skeins from Sun Valley Fibers are worth mentioning. They are so cute and teeny—perfect for all of the projects in this book! The day before I turned in my manuscript for this book, Three Fates Yarns happened to be across the aisle from me at an event where I was vending. They had the most fun mini-skeins pack (shown unlabeled in the photo above). Look at those delicious rainbow colors!

LITTLE NEEDLES

I knit all of these patterns using the Magic Loop method for working in the round because that is how I roll. I am a Magic Loop method advocate. Basically you can't talk to me for more than like 28.3 seconds without me asking if you use Magic Loop. (And that is what I actually call it, but my tech and copy editors always correct me and tell me it's

"Magic Loop method" not "Magic Loop." They say if I am getting actual "Magic" in my "Magic Loop," I am not sharing something with the rest of them.)

The Magic Loop method is just one way of working in the round. You can also use double-pointed needles, or if you have some other fancy-pants (or magical) way of working small circumference projects in the round, you can use that. You can also use both the Magic Loop method and double-pointed needles in one project if you want. I won't judge. Just go with the flow and do what works for you.

PICKING UP VERSUS KNITTING SEPARATELY

Since I wanted all of these patterns to be quick knits, I decided to write them so they could be knit in one piece to eliminate as much finishing as possible. I find finishing is what takes me the most time when knitting toys. I decided to quicken the process by knitting the main body shape and then picking up stitches for all of the limbs and other appendages. Though it may seem tricky, it really isn't that hard.

If you're uncomfortable with the whole picking-up-stitches thing, no worries! Instead of picking up, just cast on however many stitches the pattern calls for. For example, the "Basic Stitchy-Body Arm" directions (page 64) say, "Rnd 1: Using circular needle for Magic Loop method, pick up 4 sts from the neck dec rnd and 4 sts from 1 rnd below." Rather than picking up as instructed, simply cast on the eight stitches instead, and then begin with round one and knit to the end. Easy, right? This can be done for all of the limbs in this book.

Once you have all of your appendages and body finished, whipstitch the limbs to the body using a tapestry needle.

Picking Up Stitches

If you decide that picking up stitches from the body is the way you want to go, here are a few basic things to know before you start knitting. A word of caution: This isn't your typical pick up and knit, often abbreviated as "PU". In this book *pick up* is used for picking up stitches from the body as described below, and *PU* is used for the standard pick up and knit.

First of all, slide your needle through the stitches you want to pick up and have them ready to join with your working yarn on the first round. Simply slip your needle into the number of stitches called for in the pattern.

Second, unless the pattern says the limb is knit flat (not in the round), you will want to pick up stitches so they are in a "circle" to be knitted in the round. This means whatever the number of stitches to pick up is, you will want half of them on a bottom needle and half on an upper needle. Make sense?

So, if the pattern says to "pick up 3 and 3 sts," you'll start by picking up three stitches on one needle **(fig. 1)**. Then pick up the other three stitches on your second needle (this being the other end of your circular needle for Magic Loop method) **(fig. 2)**. Ta-da! Six stitches waiting on your needles to be knit in a circle.

Are you wondering where to pick up your stitches? In general, arms are picked up at the "neck." Most of the body shapes have a fairly defined neckline, but for the Basic Biscuit Body (page 51), I like to wrap my hand around the body where I want the neck to be and squeeze it so it gives me a better idea of where to aim for. Pick up legs on the bottom or base, or from the cast-on edge. Ears and horns are picked up on the top of the head, either from side to side or from front to back. Pick up tails and wings on the backs of the bodies. If you are wondering where something should go, simply reference the pictures, or use your own creativity to decide where limbs should be placed! Look for more in-depth tutorials online. See "Where to Go for Help" on page 14.

Fig. 1

Fig. 2

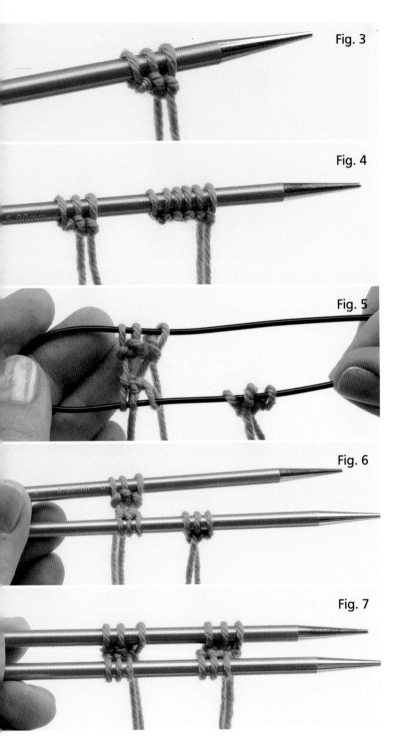

Fig. 3

Fig. 4

Fig. 5

Fig. 6

Fig. 7

Two-at-a-Time Legs

Okay, I am excited about this one. The Basic Uni-Body (page 41) is a mini version of my signature body shape where the legs and body are all knit as one piece. I have been doing legs the same way for this shape since I started writing patterns back in 2009, but I decided it was time to mix things up and try a new way of knitting legs and body as one piece. This is what I came up with, and I feel it's highly effective.

First of all, I knit this using the Magic Loop method. If you want to use double-pointed needles, put your stitches on four needles and work the stitches with the fifth needle. Okey-dokey, here we go.

You'll be working both legs at the same time, so you'll need to work either from two balls of yarn, or from the inside and the outside of a center-pull ball. The legs begin with six stitches, so start by casting on half that number (three stitches) with the first end of the yarn. These are the first three stitches of leg 1 **(fig. 3)**.

Then using your other piece of yarn, cast on all six stitches of leg 2 **(fig. 4)**.

Divide your stitches onto your two needle tips to set yourself up for working in the round. Using Magic Loop method, slide your stitches down the cable of your needle and pull the cable out through the middle of your six stitches for leg 2 **(fig. 5)**.

At this point, your front needle will have six stitches (three leg 1 stitches and three leg 2 stitches) and your back needle will have just three stitches from leg 2 **(fig. 6)**.

Grab your working yarn from leg 1 and cast on three more stitches for leg 1 onto your back needle. You'll have 12 stitches total; six on each needle **(fig. 7)**.

There you go—two legs ready to work at the same time. Now, slide the stitches on the back needle onto the cable so you can use the needle tip to join for working in the round. You'll be joining the last stitch cast on (for leg 1) with the first stitch cast on (also for leg 1) **(fig. 8)**.

To work two legs at the same time, work the first half of the stitches from leg 1 **(fig. 9)**.

Then drop that working yarn and pick up the working yarn attached to leg 2 (it will be hanging from the back set of stitches) **(fig. 10)**.

Work the first half of the stitches of leg 2 on your front needle. When you run out of stitches on that needle, rotate your work around to your back needle and work those stitches with the same yarn **(fig. 11)**.

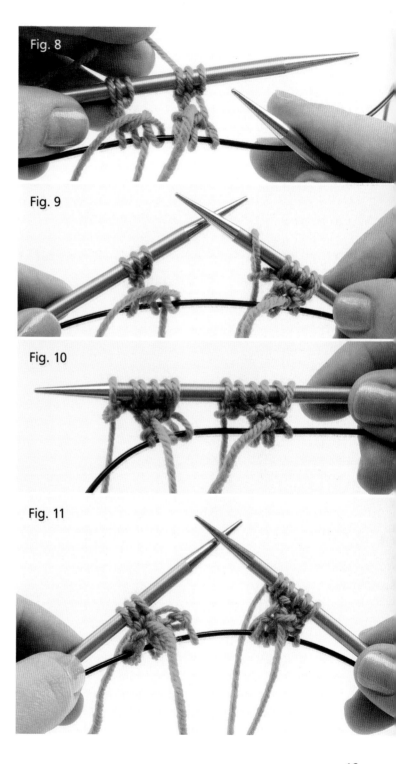

Fig. 8

Fig. 9

Fig. 10

Fig. 11

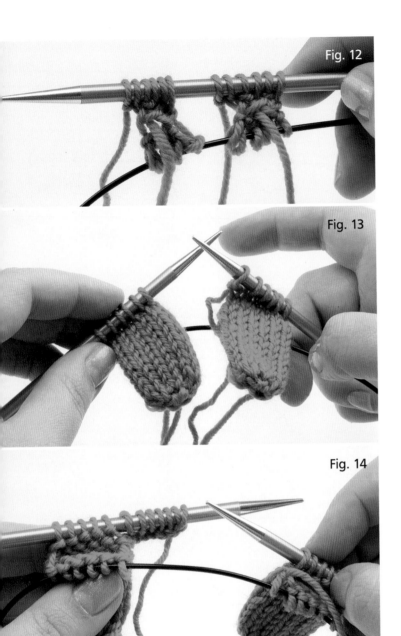

Fig. 12

Fig. 13

Fig. 14

Once you have worked through all the leg 2 stitches on your back needle, drop your working yarn from leg 2, and go back to the working yarn for leg 1, and work the rest of the leg 1 stitches. This will complete one round (**fig. 12**).

Continue working both legs like this until you have worked the 11 rounds called for. Once you get to round 12, work the first half of the leg 1 stitches (**fig. 13**).

Turn your work so you are looking at the purl side of the fabric. Continuing with the leg 1 working yarn, use the knit cast on to cast on the six stitches between the legs (**fig. 14**).

Turn your work back to the right side, and using the yarn from leg 1, knit across all 12 stitches of leg 2 (**fig. 15** on page 15).

Continuing with the same yarn, turn your work once again so that the wrong side is facing you. Use the knit cast on to cast on six stitches (**fig. 16** on page 15).

Turn your work once again and, continuing with the same yarn, knit the final six stitches of leg 1 (**fig. 17** on page 15) (36 sts).

At this point you can cut the yarn from leg 2. You'll stuff and add safety eyes later through the hole you just created here with the additional cast-on stitches.

Cool way of knitting the legs, right? I think I like it too. Check out the online tutorial (see "Where to Go for Help," below).

WHERE TO GO FOR HELP

Does a term or knitting technique still have you confused, even after my stupendous guidelines? No worries; even knitting superheroes sometimes need to ask for help! I originally had so much information and instruction for this book that I could have written a second book on just how to do everything in here. How boring would that have been? Yikes! Instead, we have compiled additional resources that are available online.

If anything in these pages has you stumped, just visit ShopMartingale.com/extras or my blog, RebeccaDanger .typepad.com, for all sorts of free downloadable instructions and how-to videos to help you out. Here are some of the techniques you'll find online.

- ⌘ Afterthought noses
- ⌘ I-cord around a pipe cleaner
- ⌘ Kitchener stitch
- ⌘ Magic Loop method
- ⌘ Making fringe
- ⌘ Making a knitted ring
- ⌘ Modified I-cord
- ⌘ Picking up stitches for ears, horns, tails, wings, noses, and beaks
- ⌘ Provisional cast on
- ⌘ Turkish cast on
- ⌘ Two-at-a-time legs

Also, remember that the Internet is your friend. There are many other places to go for help as well, like KnittingHelp.com, YouTube.com, or your local yarn shop. KnittingHelp.com offers fantastic videos to guide you every step of the way. If you search the confusing term on YouTube, there's usually a multitude of videos to help. Additionally, when you buy your supplies at a local yarn shop, they're usually more than happy to help you out with any knitting questions you might have. Local yarn shops will often have classes that may be of help to you as well; you could even ask them if they would do a class based on this book!

Alrighty, that's it for the boring parts. Now on to the patterns. Go! Get knitting!

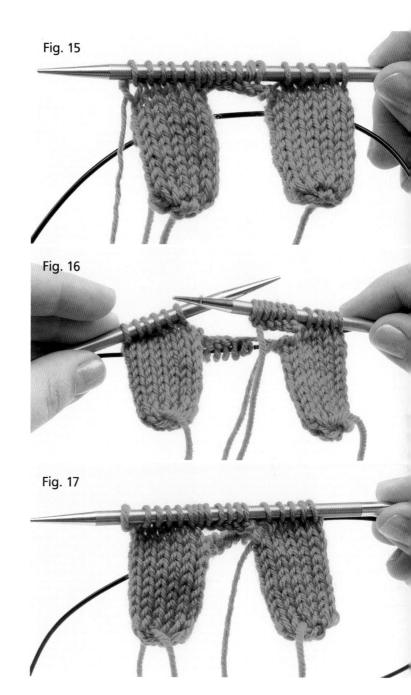

Fig. 15

Fig. 16

Fig. 17

Basic Peanut Body

I think this just might be my favorite body of all the body shapes in this book. It is tiny, and cute, and it seemed like no matter what I turned it into, I always had more than enough yardage with my 50 yards. The cute peanutty body shape looks awesome with or without limbs, sitting so the top bump is his head, or on his side for a whole new body shape. And this body is so quick to make! I could crank these guys out in like two hours by the time I finished writing this book.

I had *so* many ideas for this shape, but narrowed it down and have turned this body shape into everything from a cactus to a yak for you here. Let your imagination run wild to turn this shape into a million different creatures!

BASIC PEANUT-BODY SAMPLE

Merino Worsted from Another Crafty Girl (100% superwash merino; 100 g; 215 yds) in color Bubblegum

Approx 6½" tall from head to toe

MATERIALS

Approx 17 g (37 yds) of worsted-weight yarn 4

40" circular needle 2 or 3 sizes smaller than that recommended for your yarn (for Magic Loop method)

Size 5 (3.75 mm) circular needle

1 pair of 12 mm safety eyes

BASIC PEANUT BODY

Using circular needle for Magic Loop method, CO 6 sts and join for working in the round, making sure not to twist sts. PM to indicate beg of rnd.

Rnd 1: K1f&b around. (12 sts)

Rnd 2: (K1f&b, K1) around. (18 sts)

Rnd 3: (K1f&b, K2) around. (24 sts)

Rnd 4: (K1f&b, K3) around. (30 sts)

Rnd 5: (K1f&b, K4) around. (36 sts)

Rnds 6–19: Knit all sts.

Rnd 20: K2tog around. (18 sts)

Rnd 21: Knit all sts.

Rnd 22: (K1f&b, K1f&b, K1) around. (30 sts)

Rnds 23–30: Knit all sts.

Rnd 31: (K2tog, K1) around. (20 sts)

Rnd 32: Knit all sts.

Stop and add any eye patches, safety eyes, belly buttons, dots, or anything else you want to include now so that you can tie off all ends on the inside before you go any further. Then stuff body.

Rnd 33: K2tog around. (10 sts)

Add any last bits of stuffing, then cut yarn and using tapestry needle, thread yarn tail through rem sts to close head.

BASIC PEANUT-BODY ARM

Make 2.

Rnd 1: Using circular needle for Magic Loop method, pick up 2 sts from neck dec rnd and 2 sts from 1 rnd below (see page 11).

Rnds 2–10: Knit all sts.

Rnd 11: K1f&b around. (8 sts)

Rnds 12–14: Knit all sts.

Stuff hand. Cut yarn and use tapestry needle to thread tail through rem sts to close hand.

BASIC PEANUT-BODY LEG

Make 2.

Rnd 1: Using circular needle for Magic Loop method, pick up 3 and 3 sts from bottom of body. For both legs, be sure that beg of rnd is on *backside* of body.

Rnds 2–15: Knit all sts.

Working just first 3 sts of rnd and holding last 3 sts of rnd on your cable, work back and forth in rows as follows.

Row 1: Sl 1, knit to end. Turn.

Row 2: Sl 1, purl to end. Turn.

Work rows 1 and 2 again for a total of 4 rows, ending on a purl row.

Rnd 1 of foot: Turn your work so you're ready to knit. PM to indicate new beg of rnd. Knit across heel sts once more. Using same needle tip, PU 2 sts from LH side of heel flap. Flip to other needle tip and knit across held instep sts and PU 2 sts from RH side of heel flap. (10 sts)

Rnd 2: K3, K2tog, K3, ssk. (8 sts)

Rnds 3–7: Knit all sts.

Stuff foot. Cut yarn and use tapestry needle to thread tail through rem sts to close foot.

basic peanut body

Bitty Bee

Bzzzzzz! This cute bitty bee won't sting, but hopefully he will help you remember to stop and smell the flowers!

SAMPLE

A Rios from Malabrigo (100% pure merino superwash; 100 g; 210 yds) in color 195 Black (4)

B Rios from Malabrigo in color 96 Sunset

C Rios from Malabrigo in color 63 Natural

Approx 6" tall, from head to toe

MATERIALS

Using worsted-weight yarn, (4)

A Approx 15 g (32 yds)

B Approx 2 g (5 yds)

C Approx 5 g (11 yds)

US size 5 (3.75 mm) needles

1 pair of 12 mm safety eyes

BODY

Following instructions for Basic Peanut-Body (page 17), CO with A and work as follows.

Rnds 1–8: With A.

Rnds 9–14: With B.

Rnd 15 to end of body: With A.

LEG

Make 2.

Using A, follow instructions for "Basic Peanut-Body Leg" (page 18).

ARM

Make 2.

Rnd 1: Using A and circular needle for Magic Loop method, pick up 2 sts from neck dec rnd and 2 sts from 1 rnd below (see page 11).

Rnds 2–12: Knit all sts.

Rnd 13: K1f&b around. (8 sts)

Rnds 14–17: Knit all sts.

Stuff hand. Cut yarn and use tapestry needle to thread tail through rem sts to close hand.

WING

Make 2, knit flat (not in the round).

Row 1: Using C and any needle, pick up 7 sts from center of back in one line, starting at bottom of bee and working up toward head.

Row 2: K1f&b, K5, K1f&b. (9 sts)

Row 3: K1f&b, K7, K1f&b. (11 sts)

Row 4: K1f&b, K9, K1f&b. (13 sts)

Rows 5–13: Knit all sts.

Row 14: Ssk, knit to last 2 sts, K2tog. (11 sts)

Rep row 14 another 3 times. (5 sts)

Loosely BO all sts.

ANTENNA

Make 2.

Antennae are worked as I-cords (page 79).

Rnd 1: Using A and 1 dpn, pick up 3 sts from one side of the top of the head, setting you up to knit an I-cord.

Rnd 2: Knit all sts.

Rnd 3: K1, K2tog. (2 sts)

Rnds 4–12: Knit all sts as an I-cord. (You can also work antenna without counting rounds until it's long enough to tie in a knot.)

Cut yarn and use tapestry needle to thread tail through rem sts to close the antenna.

Tie antenna in a knot at the end.

Snack-Sized Yak

This tiny yak is perfect proof that everything is at least 1,000% cuter in small scale. Since that is the case, would a herd of 10 of these little guys make them 10,000% cuter than their big brethren?

SAMPLE

A Fizz from Crystal Palace Yarns (100% polyester; 50 g; 120 yds) in color 9152 Wood Grain (4)

B Merino 5 from Crystal Palace Yarns (100% superwash merino wool; 50 g; 110 yds) in color 5239 Dark Chocolate (4)

C Merino 5 from Crystal Palace Yarns in color 1008 Old Gold

About 8" tall, from head to toe

MATERIALS

Using worsted-weight yarn, (4)

A Approx 7 g (17 yds)

B Approx 23 g (51 yds)

C Approx 3 g (7 yds)

Waste yarn in a color different than B

US size 5 (3.75 mm) needles

1 pair of 9 mm safety eyes

BODY

Following instructions for Basic Peanut Body (page 17), CO with A and B held tog and work as follows.

Rnds 1–21: With A and B held tog.

Rnd 22: Drop A, and using just B, (K1f&b, K1f&b, K1) around. (30 sts) Cont in B to end of body.

Rnds 23 and 24: Knit all sts.

Rnd 25: K4, switch to waste yarn and knit next 7 sts in waste yarn, slip these 7 sts back to your LH needle, go back to your working yarn, and knit across waste yarn sts and to end of rnd. This rnd will become Yak's nose.

Rnd 26 to end of body: As written.

NOSE

Release 14 held sts by slipping 7 top and 7 bottom sts to your needle tips and removing waste yarn.

Rnd 1: Using B, (K7, PU 1 st from gap between top and bottom) twice. (16 sts)

Rnd 2: (K1f&b, K6, K1f&b) twice. (20 sts)

Rnds 3–7: Knit all sts.

Rnd 8: K2tog around. (10 sts)

Rnd 9: Knit all sts.

Rnd 10: K2tog around. (5 sts)

Stuff nose. Cut yarn and use tapestry needle to thread tail through rem sts to close nose.

ARM

Make 2.

Rnd 1: Using B and circular needle for Magic Loop method, pick up 3 sts from neck dec rnd and 3 sts from 1 rnd below (see page 11).

Rnds 2–20: Knit all sts.

Rnd 21: K1f&b around. (12 sts)

Rnds 22–26: Knit all sts.

Rnd 27: K2tog around. (6 sts)

Stuff hand. Cut yarn and use tapestry needle to thread tail through rem sts to close hand.

LEG

Make 2.

Rnd 1: Using B and circular needle for Magic Loop method, pick up 4 and 4 sts from bottom edge of body. For both legs, be sure that beg of rnd is on *backside* of body.

Rnds 2–25: Knit all sts.

Working just first 4 sts of rnd and holding last 4 sts of rnd on your cable, work back and forth as follows.

Row 1: Sl 1, knit to end. Turn.

Row 2: Sl 1, purl to end. Turn.

Work rows 1 and 2 for a total of 4 rows, ending on a purl row.

Rnd 1 of foot: Turn your work so you're ready to knit. PM to indicate new beg of rnd. Knit across heel sts once more. Using same needle tip, PU 3 sts from LH side of heel flap (2 gusset sts plus 1 st in gap). Flip to other needle tip and knit across held instep sts and PU 3 sts from RH side of heel flap (2 gusset sts plus 1 st in gap). (14 sts)

Rnd 2: K4, K2tog, K6, ssk. (12 sts)

Rnd 3: Knit all sts.

Rnd 4: K4, K2tog, K4, ssk. (10 sts)

Rnds 5–9: Knit all sts.

Rnd 10: K2tog around. (5 sts)

Stuff foot. Cut yarn and use tapestry needle to thread tail through rem sts to close foot.

HORN

Make 2.

Rnd 1: Using C and circular needle for Magic Loop method, pick up 3 and 3 sts from front to back on one side of top of head.

Rnds 2–12: Knit all sts.

Rnd 13: K2tog around. (3 sts)

Rnd 14: Knit all sts.

Stuff horn. (It can help to use chopstick or eraser end of a pencil.) Cut yarn and use tapestry needle to thread tail through rem sts to close horn.

Referring to photo on page 20, tack down about halfway along bottom of horn to head below.

EAR

Make 2, knit flat (not in the round).

Row 1: Using B and circular needle, pick up 3 sts in a straight line from right below horn. Be sure RS faces up and WS faces down toward head.

Row 2: Purl all sts.

Row 3: K1, K1f&b, K1. (4 sts)

Row 4: Purl all sts.

Row 5: K1, K1f&b in next 2 sts, K1. (6 sts)

Rows 6–8: Work in St st (knit on RS, purl on WS).

Row 9: K1, ssk, K2tog, K1. (4 sts)

Row 10: P2tog twice. (2 sts)

Cut yarn and use tapestry needle to thread tail through rem sts to finish ear.

Bitsy-Bot

Technology these days seems to keep getting smaller and smaller. This little guy sure fits right in with the most modern tiny technology!

SAMPLE

A Rios from Malabrigo (100% pure merino superwash; 100 g; 210 yds) in color 43 Plomo (4)

B Rios from Malabrigo in color 611 Ravelry Red

About 6" tall, from head to toe (not including antenna)

MATERIALS

Using worsted-weight yarn, [4]

A   Approx 17 g (36 yds)

B   Approx 4 g (9 yds)

US size 5 (3.75 mm) needles

1 pair of 12mm safety eyes

2" piece of pipe cleaner, any color

BODY

Following instructions for Basic Peanut Body (page 17), CO with A and work as follows.

Rnds 1–6: With A.

Rnds 7–9: With B.

Rnd 10 to end of body: With A.

ANTENNA

Rnd 1: Using B and circular needle for Magic Loop method, pick up 2 and 2 sts (see page 11) from center of head. Insert a pipe cleaner into top of head in center of picked up sts and sticking up so you can knit I-cord around it. See "Where to Go for Help" on page 14.

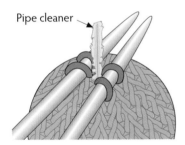

Pipe cleaner

Stitches picked up and pipe cleaner inserted.

Rnds 2–6: Knit all sts.

Cut pipe cleaner flush with last rnd knit.

Rnd 7: K1f&b around. (8 sts)

Rnds 8–12: Knit all sts.

Stuff bobble. Cut yarn and use tapestry needle to thread tail through rem sts to finish antenna.

ARM

Make 2.

Rnd 1: Using A and circular needle for Magic Loop method, pick up 3 sts from neck dec rnd and 3 sts from 1 rnd below. For both arms, be sure that beg of rnd is on underside of arm, closest to body.

Rnds 2–17: Knit all sts.

Rnd 18: K1f&b in first 3 sts of rnd, knit to end. (9 sts)

Rnds 19–23: Knit all sts.

Rnd 24: K2tog around, ending K1. (5 sts)

Stuff hand. Cut yarn and use tapestry needle to thread tail through rem sts to close hand.

LEG

Make 2.

Rnd 1: Using A and circular needle for Magic Loop method, pick up 4 and 4 sts from bottom of body. For both legs, be sure that beg of rnd is on *backside* of body.

Rnds 2–18: Knit all sts.

Working just first 4 sts of rnd and holding last 4 sts of rnd on your cable, work back and forth as follows.

Row 1: Sl 1, knit to end. Turn.

Row 2: Sl 1, purl to end. Turn.

Work rows 1 and 2 for a total of 6 rows, ending on a purl row.

Rnd 1 of foot: Turn your work so you're ready to knit. PM to indicate new beg of rnd. Knit across heel sts once more. Using same needle tip, PU 4 sts from LH side of heel flap (3 gusset sts plus 1 st in gap). Flip to other needle tip and knit across held instep sts and PU 4 sts from RH side of heel flap (3 gusset sts plus 1 st in gap). (16 sts)

Rnd 2: K4, K2tog, K8, ssk. (14 sts)

Rnd 3: Knit all sts.

Rnd 4: K4, K2tog, K6, ssk. (12 sts)

Rnds 5–9: Knit all sts.

Rnd 10: K2tog around. (6 sts)

Stuff foot. Cut yarn and use tapestry needle to thread tail through rem sts to close foot.

Cutie Cactus

Ever had bad luck keeping plants alive? Do people joke you can't even keep a cactus alive? Well, here's one plant even the blackest of thumbs can keep healthy and happy!

SAMPLE

A Rios from Malabrigo (100% pure merino superwash; 100 g; 210 yds) in color 37 Lettuce 4

B Rios from Malabrigo in color 63 Natural

C Rios from Malabrigo in color 96 Sunset

About 4" tall

MATERIALS

Using worsted-weight yarn, 4

A Approx 16 g (34 yds)

B Approx 6 g (13 yds)

C Approx 5 g (11 yds)

US size 5 (3.75 mm) needles

1 pair of 12 mm safety eyes

BODY

Using A, work body following instructions for Basic Peanut Body (page 17).

LEFT ARM

Rnd 1: Using A and circular needle for Magic Loop method, starting near head and working downward, pick up 8 sts, then slide those sts down the cable to other needle tip and pick up 8 from bottom to top (see page 11). Be sure that beg of rnd starts at top of body. (16 sts)

Rnd 2: K1f&b, K5, K2tog, ssk, knit to last st, K1f&b. (16 sts)

Rnd 3: K1f&b, knit to last st, K1f&b. (18 sts)

Rnd 4: K1f&b, K6, K2tog, ssk, knit to last st, K1f&b. (18 sts)

Rnd 5: K1f&b, knit to last st, K1f&b. (20 sts)

Rnd 6: K1f&b, K7, K2tog, ssk, knit to last st, K1f&b. (20 sts)

Rnd 7: K1f&b, knit to last st, K1f&b. (22 sts)

Rnds 8 and 9: Knit all sts.

Rnd 10: (Ssk, K7, K2tog) twice. (18 sts)

Rnd 11: (Ssk, K5, K2tog) twice. (14 sts)

Rnd 12: (Ssk, K3, K2tog) twice. (10 sts)

Rnd 13: (Ssk, K1, K2tog) twice. (6 sts)

Add a little bit of stuffing to arm. Cut yarn and use tapestry needle to thread tail through rem sts to close arm.

RIGHT ARM

To make slightly offset arms like the sample, be sure bottom picked-up st is at same level as left arm.

Rnd 1: Using A and circular needle for Magic Loop method, starting near head and 1 stitch lower than on left, work downward to pick up 7 sts, then slide those sts down the cable to other needle tip and pick up 7 from bottom to top. Be sure that beg of rnd starts at top of body. (14 sts)

Rnd 2: K1f&b, K4, K2tog, ssk, knit to last st, K1f&b. (14 sts)

Rnd 3: K1f&b, knit to last st, K1f&b. (16 sts)

Rnd 4: K1f&b, K5, K2tog, ssk, knit to last st, K1f&b. (16 sts)

Rnd 5: K1f&b, knit to last st, K1f&b. (18 sts)

Rnd 6: K1f&b, K6, K2tog, ssk, knit to last st, K1f&b. (18 sts)

Rnd 7: K1f&b, knit to last st, K1f&b. (20 sts)

Rnds 8 and 9: Knit all sts.

Rnd 10: (Ssk, K6, K2tog) twice. (16 sts)

Rnd 11: (Ssk, K4, K2tog) twice. (12 sts)

Rnd 12: (Ssk, K2, K2tog) twice. (8 sts)

Add a little bit of stuffing to arm. Cut yarn and use tapestry needle to thread tail through rem sts to close arm.

FLOWER

Make 5 petals and join them in flower center.

Petal

Make 5.

Using B and your circular needle, CO 3 sts. DO NOT JOIN.

Row 1: Knit all sts.

Row 2: K1f&b, K1, K1f&b. (5 sts)

Rows 3–5: Knit all sts.

Cut yarn and place sts on st holder, or leave on cable of circular needle as you make rem 4 petals.

Flower Center

With all 5 petals on cable of your needle, switch to C.

Rnd 1: K2tog across the first 2 petals. Knit first 2 sts of 3rd petal tog, then slide sts across cable to back needle to set yourself up to work in the round using Magic Loop method. K2tog across rest of petals to last 3 sts, K3tog. (12 sts)

Rnd 2: Join across needle tips for working in the rnd using Magic Loop method, and knit all sts.

Rnd 3: K2tog around. (6 sts)

Cut yarn and use tapestry needle to thread tail through rem sts to close the center of flower.

FINISHING

Sew flower to one side of top of cactus's head. Using about 6" lengths of A, make fringe (see "Making Fringe," right) in a random pattern on body and spines of cactus. Trim fringe short (½"-long or less) to make spines on body.

Making Fringe

Making fringe is easy. Cut pieces of yarn the required length. Thread both ends of the yarn through the eye of a tapestry needle. Pull the needle through the spot where you want fringe until the full needle has pulled through and you start to see the loop end of your yarn. Once you see the loop, you can slip your needle off the yarn. Then thread the ends of the yarn through the loop and pull it tight. Trim as needed to desired length.

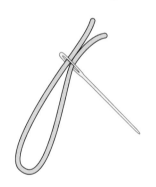

basic peanut body

Itty-Bitty Batty

Here is yet another case where tiny makes things so much better. To be honest, real bats give me the heebie-jeebies, but this tiny version gives me the warm fuzzies because he is so teeny, cute, and cuddly! And he is the best ever for all of your Halloween decorating and party needs. Be sure to check out my awesome "Bat Mobile" (page 75).

SAMPLE

Superwash Worsted from SweetGeorgia Yarns (100% superwash merino wool; 115 g; 200 yds) in color Charcoal (4)

About 4½" tall, from ears to toes

MATERIALS

Approx 25 g (44 yds) of worsted-weight yarn (4)

US size 5 (3.75 mm) needles

1 pair of 12 mm safety eyes

BODY

Work body following instructions for Basic Peanut Body (page 17).

WING

Make 2.

Rnd 1: Using circular needle for Magic Loop method, starting near head and working downward, pick up 13 sts, then slide those sts down the cable to other needle tip and pick up 13 from bottom to top (see page 11). Be sure that beg of rnd starts at top of body.

Rnd 2: Knit all sts.

Rnd 3: Knit to last 2 sts on your first needle tip, K2tog, ssk first 2 sts on second needle tip, then knit all sts to end of rnd.

Rnd 4: Knit all sts.

Rnds 5–10: Rep rnds 3 and 4 three more times. (18 sts at end of rnd 10)

Rnds 11–15: Rep rnd 3 five times. (8 sts at end of rnd 15)

Rnd 16: K2tog around. (4 sts)

Rnd 17: Knit all sts.

Rnd 18: (K1f&b, K1) twice. (6 sts)

Rnds 19–21: Knit all sts.

Add a little bit of stuffing to hand. Cut yarn and use tapestry needle to thread tail through rem sts to close wing.

EAR

Make 2.

Rnd 1: Using circular needle for Magic Loop method, pick up 4 and 4 sts from one side of top of head, working from center to side.

Rnds 2 and 3: Knit all sts

Rnd 4: (K1, K2tog, K1) twice. (6 sts)

Rnd 5: Knit all sts.

Cut yarn and use tapestry needle to thread tail through rem sts to close ear.

FOOT

Make 2.

Rnd 1: Using circular needle for Magic Loop method, pick up 3 and 3 sts from bottom of body.

Rnds 2 and 3: Knit all sts.

Rnd 4: (K1, K1f&b, K1) twice. (8 sts)

Rnd 5: Knit all sts.

Rnd 6: (K1, K1f&b, K2) twice. (10 sts)

Rnds 7–9: Knit all sts.

Stuff foot. Cut yarn and use tapestry needle to thread tail through rem sts to close foot.

basic peanut body

Junior Jackalope

Oh good gravy, how much do you love this little fella? Just when I thought jackalopes couldn't get any better, this little guy came into my life and blew all other jackalopes out of the water. I do believe that life may not get any better than when holding a tiny jackalope in the palm of your hands. Call me crazy, but when you knit one for yourself, you'll understand exactly what I mean!

SAMPLE

A Shepherd Worsted from Lorna's Laces (100% superwash merino wool; 4 oz; 225 yds) in color 511 Buckingham Fountain 【4】

B Shepherd Worsted from Lorna's Laces in color 611 Magnificent Mile

C Shepherd Worsted from Lorna's Laces in color 0ns Natural

About 7½" tall, from antlers to toes

MATERIALS

Using worsted-weight yarn, 【4】

A Approx 20 g (40 yds)

B Approx 2 g (4 yds)

C Approx 3 g (6 yds)

US size 5 (3.75 mm) needles

1 pair of 9 mm safety eyes

15 mm safety nose

BODY

Using A, work body following instructions for Basic Peanut Body (page 17).

ARM

Make 2.

Rnd 1: Using A and circular needle for Magic Loop method, pick up 3 sts from the dec rnd and 3 sts from 1 rnd below (see page 11).

Rnds 2 and 3: Knit all sts

Rnd 4: (K1f&b, K2) twice. (8 sts)

Rnds 5 and 6: Knit all sts.

Rnd 7: (K3, K1f&b) twice. (10 sts)

Rnds 8–16: Knit all sts.

Stuff hand. Cut yarn and use tapestry needle to thread tail through rem sts to close hand.

LEG

Make 2.

Rnd 1: Using A and circular needle for Magic Loop method, pick up 4 and 4 sts from bottom of body.

Rnds 2 and 3: Knit all sts.

Rnd 4: (K1f&b, K3) twice. (10 sts)

Rnds 5 and 6: Knit all sts.

Rnd 7: (K4, K1f&b) twice. (12 sts)

Rnds 8–18: Knit all sts.

Rnd 19: K2tog around. (6 sts)

Stuff foot. Cut yarn and use tapestry needle to thread tail through rem sts to close foot.

EAR

Make 2.

Rnd 1: Using A and circular needle for Magic Loop method, pick up 3 and 3 sts from one side of top of head, working from center to side. Be sure to leave room for antlers between where you pick up sts for ears.

Rnd 2: (K1, K1f&b, K1) twice. (8 sts)

Rnds 3–14: Knit all sts.

Cut yarn and use tapestry needle to thread tail through rem sts to close ear.

ANTLER

Make 1 and 1 reversed.

Antlers are worked as I-cords (see "Abbreviations and Glossary" on page 79).

Rnd 1: Using B and 1 dpn, pick up 4 sts from one side between ears on top of head, setting you up to knit an I-cord.

Rnds 2–14: Knit all sts as an I-cord.

Cut yarn and pull tail through rem sts to close antler.

Work side antler.

Rnd 1: About halfway up the antler (I started in rnd 6 of antler), and starting on side of antler nearest to ear (pointing out from center of head), use B to pick up 4 sts with 1 dpn, setting you up again to knit an I-cord.

Rnds 2–6: Knit all sts as an I-cord.

Cut yarn and pull tail through rem sts to close side antler.

TAIL

Rnd 1: Using C and circular needle for Magic Loop method, pick up 4 and 4 sts from bottom center of back of body.

Rnd 2: K1f&b around. (16 sts)

Rnd 3: Knit all sts.

Rnd 4: (K1f&b, K1) around. (24 sts)

Rnds 5–8: Knit all sts.

Rnd 9: (K2tog, K1) around. (16 sts)

Rnd 10: Knit all sts.

Rnd 11: K2tog around. (8 sts)

Stuff tail. Cut yarn and use tapestry needle to thread tail through rem sts to close tail.

Modified I-Cord

If you don't like Magic Loop method, I did figure out a nifty way of working in the round with two double-pointed needles that I coined "modified I-cord." Since I wrote the patterns so all the limbs are picked up and knit right from the bodies, I found trying to pick up four to six stitches with three double-pointed needles a little too annoying (hence why they're all done with Magic Loop method). Use modified I-cord knitting and all problems are fixed. OK, not all problems, but annoying 3-dpn-knitty-picky-uppy-whatever problems are fixed.

All you do is use two double-pointed needles to hold your stitches and use a third double-pointed needle to knit with, rather than the traditional stitches on three or four double-pointed needles. Kinda like Magic Loop Method without the cable, right? I know; I am loving it. You can find out more on my video tutorial online. See "Where To Go For Help" on page 14.

basic peanut body

Basic Bowling-Pin Body

There is just something about the bowling-pin shape that I love. A slightly undersized head atop a slightly oversized tummy—it has a certain *je ne sais quoi*. That is, if little knitted creatures can possess *je ne sais quoi*. My vote is that they can.

My original design includes a round base that you pick up and knit once you finish the body; this lets him sit up nice and straight on his own (something knitted critters often don't like to do without a lot of coaxing and creative thinking). However, once I got knitting, I found this shape looked just as awesome and even a little different if you omit the base and sew the cast-on edge shut at the end for a flat bottom. I found this very helpful on a few patterns, like Small-Peanuts Elephant (page 32), which took a bit more than my intended 50 yards of yarn.

Whatever look you love, I feel like this shape offers a huge variety of ways to be creative and go beyond my patterns to make your own little knitted critters!

BASIC BOWLING-PIN-BODY SAMPLE

Rios from Malabrigo (100% pure merino superwash; 100 g; 210 yds) in color 227 Volcano (4)

About 8" tall, from head to toe

MATERIALS

Approx 23 g (50 yds) of worsted-weight yarn (4)

40" circular needle 2 or 3 sizes smaller than that recommended for your yarn (for Magic Loop method)

US size 5 (3.75 mm) needles

1 pair of 12 mm safety eyes

Pattern Note

This body is designed with a base that is picked up after the body is knit. It will use only a small amount of yarn. If you have less than 50 yards of yarn, it's easy to stretch your yardage further by using a contrasting color for the base. Or skip the base entirely and sew the cast-on edge together to create a flat seam on the bottom.

BASIC BOWLING-PIN BODY

Using circular needle for Magic Loop method, CO 36 sts and join for working in the round, making sure not to twist sts. PM to indicate beg of rnd.

Rnds 1–12: Knit all sts.

Rnd 13: (Ssk, K14, K2tog) twice. (32 sts)

Rnds 14 and 15: Knit all sts.

Rnd 16: (Ssk, K12, K2tog) twice. (28 sts)

Rnds 17 and 18: Knit all sts.

Rnd 19: (Ssk, K10, K2tog) twice. (24 sts)

Rnds 20 and 21: Knit all sts.

Rnd 22: (Ssk, K8, K2tog) twice. (20 sts)

Rnds 23 and 24: Knit all sts.

Rnd 25: (K1f&b, K3, K1f&b, K4, K1f&b) twice. (26 sts)

Rnd 26: Knit all sts.

Rnd 27: (K1f&b, K5, K1f&b, K5, K1f&b) twice. (32 sts)

Rnds 28–36: Knit all sts.

Rnd 37: (K2tog, K2) around. (24 sts)

Rnd 38: Knit all sts.

Rnd 39: (K2tog, K1) around. (16 sts)

Rnd 40: Knit all sts.

Rnd 41: K2tog around. (8 sts)

Cut yarn and use tapestry needle to thread tail through rem sts to close head.

BASIC BOWLING-PIN-BODY BASE

Rnd 1: Using circular needle for Magic Loop method, PU 36 sts from CO edge of body.

Rnd 2: Knit all sts in the round.

Rnd 3: (K2tog, K2) around. (27 sts)

Rnd 4: Knit all sts.

Rnd 5: (K2tog, K1) around. (18 sts)

Rnd 6: Knit all sts.

Add safety eyes and any patches or embroidery you want tied off inside body. Stuff body.

Rnd 7: K2tog around. (9 sts)

Cut yarn and use tapestry needle to thread tail through rem sts to close base.

BASIC BOWLING-PIN-BODY ARM

Make 2.

Rnd 1: Using circular needle for Magic Loop method, pick up 3 sts from neck dec rnd and 3 sts from 1 rnd below (see page 11).

Rnds 2–15: Knit all sts.

Rnd 16: (K1f&b, K1, K1f&b) twice. (10 sts)

Rnds 17–21: Knit all sts.

Stuff hand. Cut yarn and use tapestry needle to thread tail through rem sts to close hand.

BASIC BOWLING-PIN-BODY LEG

Make 2.

Rnd 1: Using circular needle for Magic Loop method, pick up 4 and 4 sts from bottom of body. For both legs, be sure that beg of rnd is on *backside* of body.

Rnds 2–19: Knit all sts.

Working just first 4 sts of rnd and holding last 4 sts of rnd on your cable, work back and forth as follows.

Row 1: Sl 1, knit to end. Turn.

Row 2: Sl 1, purl to end. Turn.

Work rows 1 and 2 for a total of 4 rows, ending on a purl row.

Rnd 1 of foot: Turn your work so you're ready to knit. PM to indicate new beg of rnd. Knit across heel sts once more. Using same needle tip, PU 3 sts (2 slipped plus 1 st in gap) from LH side of heel flap. Flip to other needle tip and knit across held instep sts and PU 3 sts (2 slipped plus 1 st in gap) from RH side of heel flap. (14 sts)

Rnd 2: K4, K2tog, K6, ssk. (12 sts)

Rnd 3: Knit all sts.

Rnd 4: K4, K2tog, K4, ssk. (10 sts)

Rnds 5–9: Knit all sts.

Rnd 10: K2tog around. (5 sts)

Stuff foot. Cut yarn and use tapestry needle to thread tail through rem sts to close foot.

basic bowling-pin body

Runty Raccoon

Though I find real raccoons terrifying (one came to our back door once, and I swear he was trying to figure out how to get into our house so he could harass us all in our sleep), their masked faces and stripey tails speak to the type of things I love in knitting. This guy is no different and every time I look at that little masked face, I think to myself, "Something this cute can't have such a scary real-life cousin, can it?"

SAMPLE

A   Rios from Malabrigo (100% pure merino superwash; 100 g; 210 yds) in color 43 Plomo (4)

B   Rios from Malabrigo in color 195 Black

C   Rios from Malabrigo in color 131 Sand Bank

About 9" tall, from head to toe

MATERIALS

Using worsted-weight yarn, (4)

A   Approx 23 g (50 yds)

B   Approx 3 g (7 yds)

C   Approx 3 g (7 yds)

US size 5 (3.75 mm) needles

1 pair of 9 mm safety eyes

18 mm safety nose

BODY

Following instructions for Basic Bowling-Pin Body (page 29), CO with A and work as follows.

Rnds 1–31: With A.

Rnds 32–34: With B.

Rnd 35 to end of body: With A.

LEG

Make 2.

Rnd 1: Using A and circular needle for Magic Loop method, from bottom edge, pick up 4 sts from front CO edge and 4 sts from back CO edge (see page 11). For both legs, be sure that beg of rnd is on *backside* of body.

Rnds 2–20: Knit all sts.

Working just first 4 sts of rnd and holding last 4 sts of rnd on your cable, work back and forth as follows.

Row 1: Sl 1, knit to end. Turn.

Row 2: Sl 1, purl to end. Turn.

Work rows 1 and 2 for a total of 6 rows, ending on a purl row.

Rnd 1 of foot: Turn your work so you're ready to knit. PM to indicate new beg of rnd. Knit across heel sts once more. Using same needle tip, PU 4 sts from LH side of heel flap (3 gusset sts plus 1 st in gap). Flip to other needle tip and knit across held instep sts and PU 4 sts from RH side of heel flap (3 gusset sts plus 1 st in gap). (16 sts)

Rnd 2: K4, K2tog, K8, ssk. (14 sts)

Rnd 3: Knit all sts.

Rnd 4: K4, K2tog, K6, ssk. (12 sts)

Rnds 5–10: Knit all sts.

Rnd 11: K2tog to end (6 sts)

Stuff foot. Cut yarn and use tapestry needle to thread tail through rem sts to close foot. Once legs have been knit, stuff body and add eyes and nose, then whipstitch base closed between legs.

ARM

Make 2.

Rnd 1: Using A and circular needle for Magic Loop method, pick up 3 sts from neck dec rnd and 3 sts from 1 rnd below. For both arms, be sure that beg of rnd is on *underside* of arm, closest to body.

Rnds 2–18: Knit all sts.

Rnd 19: K1f&b in next 3 sts, knit to end. (9 sts)

Rnds 20–25: Knit all sts.

Stuff hand. Cut yarn and use tapestry needle to thread tail through rem sts to close hand.

EAR

Make 2.

Rnd 1: Using A and circular needle for Magic Loop method, pick up 4

and 4 sts (see page 11) from one side of top of head.

Rnds 2 and 3: Knit all sts.

Rnd 4: (K1, K2tog, K1) twice. (6 sts)

Rnd 5: Knit all sts.

Cut yarn and use tapestry needle to thread tail through rem sts to close ear.

TAIL

The tail is worked in stripe pattern: 3 rnds C, 3 rnds B.

Rnd 1: Using C and circular needle for Magic Loop method, pick up 5 and 5 sts the bottom center of back of body.

Rnds 2 and 3: Knit all sts.

Rnd 4: (K1f&b, K3, K1f&b) twice. (14 sts)

Rnds 5 and 6: Knit all sts.

Rnd 7: (K1f&b, K5, K1f&b) twice. (18 sts)

Rnds 8–21: Knit all sts.

Rnd 22: K2tog around. (9 sts)

Rnd 23: Knit all sts.

Rnd 24: K2tog around, ending K1. (5 sts)

Stuff tail. Cut yarn and use tapestry needle to thread tail through rem sts to close tail.

Small-Peanuts Elephant

I love elephants and this adorable guy shows you why! I feel this is more proof that the tinier the critter, the cuter they become.

SAMPLE

A Superwash Worsted from SweetGeorgia Yarns (100% superwash merino wool; 115 g; 200 yds) in color Silver 〖4〗

B Superwash Worsted from SweetGeorgia Yarns in color Pistachio

About 8½" tall, from head to toe

basic bowling-pin body

MATERIALS

Using worsted-weight yarns, **4**

A   Approx 31 g (54 yds)

B   Approx 13 g (23 yds)

US size 5 (3.75 mm) needles

1 pair of 9 mm safety eyes

BODY

Following instructions for Basic Bowling-Pin Body (page 29), CO with A and work as follows.

Rnds 1–4: With A.

Rnds 5–23: With B.

Rnd 24 to end of body: With A.

EAR

Make 2.

Rnd 1: Using A and circular needle for Magic Loop method, starting near top of head and working downward, pick up 9 sts, then slide those sts down the cable to other needle tip and pick up 9 from bottom to top (see page 11). Be sure that beg of rnd starts at top of head.

Rnd 2: (K1f&b, K7, K1f&b) twice. (22 sts)

Rnd 3: Knit all sts.

Rnd 4: (K1f&b, K9, K1f&b) twice. (26 sts)

Rnd 5: Knit all sts.

Rnd 6: K12, K1f&b in next 2 sts, knit to end of rnd. (28 sts)

Rnds 7–9: Knit all sts.

Rnd 10: (Ssk, K10, K2tog) twice. (24 sts)

Rnd 11: (Ssk, K8, K2tog) twice. (20 sts)

Rnd 12: (Ssk, K6, K2tog) twice. (16 sts)

Rnd 13: (Ssk, K4, K2tog) twice. (12 sts)

Rnd 14: (Ssk, K2, K2tog) twice. (8 sts)

Cut yarn and use tapestry needle to thread tail through rem sts to close ear.

TRUNK

Rnd 1: Using A and circular needle for Magic Loop method, pick up 4 and 4 sts from center of face. It is helpful to add safety eyes first, and then pick up sts for trunk.

Rnds 2–25: Knit all sts.

BO all sts.

ARM

Make 2.

Rnd 1: Using B and circular needle for Magic Loop method, pick up 3 sts from last rnd of B at neck and 3 sts from 1 rnd below.

Rnds 2 and 3: Knit all sts.

Rnd 4: (K1f&b, K2) twice. (8 sts)

Rnds 5 and 6: Knit all sts.

Rnd 7: (K3, K1f&b) twice. (10 sts)

Rnds 8 and 9: Knit all sts.

Rnd 10: (K1f&b, K4) twice. (12 sts)

Rnds 11 and 12: Knit all sts.

Rnd 13: (K5, K1f&b) twice. (14 sts)

Rnds 14–20: Knit all sts, changing to A on rnd 16 for remainder of arm.

Rnd 21: K2tog around. (7 sts)

Stuff hand. Cut yarn and use tapestry needle to thread tail through rem sts to close hand.

LEG

Make 2.

Rnd 1: Using A and circular needle for Magic Loop method, from bottom edge of body, pick up 4 sts from front CO edge and 4 sts from back CO edge.

Rnds 2 and 3: Knit all sts.

Rnd 4: (K1f&b, K3) twice. (10 sts)

Rnds 5 and 6: Knit all sts.

Rnd 7: (K4, K1f&b) twice. (12 sts)

Rnds 8 and 9: Knit all sts.

Rnd 10: (K1f&b, K5) twice. (14 sts)

Rnds 11 and 12: Knit all sts.

Rnd 13: (K6, K1f&b) twice. (16 sts)

Rnds 14–20: Knit all sts.

Rnd 21: K2tog around. (8 sts)

Stuff leg. Cut yarn and use tapestry needle to thread tail through rem sts to close leg. Stuff body and add eyes, then whipstitch base closed between legs.

Mini Monster Bowling

How fun is this little game? My son Presley absolutely loved throwing the ball at the monster pins to knock them over, to the point where I had to make him his own set since I didn't think I could leave him without his new favorite game! Think of how cute and fun they would be with more pins in a super-bulky yarn. I'm just sayin'!

A   Superwash Worsted from SweetGeorgia Yarns (100% super-wash merino wool; 115 g; 200 yds) in color Snapdragon (4)

B   Superwash Worsted from SweetGeorgia Yarns in color Peashoot

C   Superwash Worsted from SweetGeorgia Yarns in color Midnight Garden

D   Superwash Worsted from SweetGeorgia Yarns in color Charcoal

Pins are about 7" tall; ball is about 3½" diameter

MATERIALS

Using worsted-weight yarn, (4)

A, B, C   Approx 25 g (44 yds) of each

D   Approx 15 g (25 yds)

Scrap of white worsted-weight yarn (1 or 2 g/2 yds)

US size 5 (3.75 mm) needles

3 pairs of 12 mm safety eyes

BODY

Make 3, one each in A, B, and C.

Using circular needle for Magic Loop method, CO 36 sts and join for working in the round, making sure not to twist sts. PM to indicate beg of rnd.

To make toothless pin, simply knit rnds 36 and 37 rather than binding off.

Rnds 1–15: Knit all sts.

Rnd 16: (Ssk, K14, K2tog) twice. (32 sts)

Rnds 17 and 18: Knit all sts.

Rnd 19: (Ssk, K12, K2tog) twice. (28 sts)

Rnds 20 and 21: Knit all sts.

Rnd 22: (Ssk, K10, K2tog) twice. (24 sts)

Rnds 23 and 24: Knit all sts.

Rnd 25: (Ssk, K8, K2tog) twice. (20 sts)

Rnds 26–32: Knit all sts.

Rnd 33: (K1f&b, K3, K1f&b, K4, K1f&b) twice. (26 sts)

Rnd 34: Knit all sts.

Rnd 35: (K1f&b, K5, K1f&b, K5, K1f&b) twice. (32 sts)

Rnd 36: Loosely BO first 16 sts of rnd, then knit to end of rnd. (16 sts)

Rnd 37: PU 1 st in just back loop of each of 16 sts bound off in previous rnd, then knit to end of rnd. (32 sts) These 2 rnds will create mouth.

Rnds 38–44: Knit all sts.

Rnd 45: (K2tog, K2) around. (24 sts)

Rnd 46: Knit all sts.

Rnd 47: (K2tog, K1) around. (16 sts)

Rnd 48: Knit all sts.

basic bowling-pin body

Rnd 49: K2tog around. (8 sts)

Cut yarn and use tapestry needle to thread tail through rem sts to close pin.

BODY BASE

Work base following instructions for "Basic Bowling-Pin-Body Base" (page 30).

TEETH

For first tooth, with head facing down, count from edge to 6th st (from monster's left side) of mouth. Beg in 6th st, use white yarn to PU 3 sts in 6th through 4th sts.

Knit 4 rows (garter st).

BO all sts.

To make a second tooth, count in 4 sts from opposite side and beg in that st, PU 3 sts and work as for first tooth.

For felt teeth, see "Felt Monster Teeth," far right.

BALL

Using D and circular needle for Magic Loop method, use Turkish CO (see "Where to Go for Help" on page 14) to CO 8 sts. Join for working in the round. PM to indicate beg of rnd.

Rnd 1: Knit all sts.

Rnd 2: K1f&b around. (16 sts)

Rnd 3: Knit all sts.

Rnd 4: (K1f&b, K1) around. (24 sts)

Rnd 5: Knit all sts.

Rnd 6: (K1f&b, K2) around. (32 sts)

Rnd 7: Knit all sts.

Rnd 8: (K1f&b, K3) around. (40 sts)

Rnd 9: Knit all sts.

Rnd 10: (K1f&b, K4) around. (48 sts)

Rnds 11–22: Knit all sts.

Rnd 23: (K2tog, K4) around. (40 sts)

Rnd 24: Knit all sts.

Rnd 25: (K2tog, K3) around. (32 sts)

Rnd 26: Knit all sts.

Rnd 27: (K2tog, K2) around. (24 sts)

Rnd 28: Knit all sts.

Rnd 29: (K2tog, K1) around. (16 sts)

Rnd 30: K2tog around. (8 sts)

Stuff bowling ball. Cut yarn and use tapestry needle to thread tail through rem sts to close ball.

Felt Monster Teeth

There are several ways to make teeth, but my favorite (and "signature" style for my monsters) is to make teeth out of white felt. Using your monster's face as a gauge for width, cut a rectangle of white felt, making sure to cut one long edge super straight. Then, using extra-sharp scissors, cut up and down at angles on the not-as-straight edge to create little pointy teeth. Be careful not to cut too far down between the teeth or the felt will want to pull apart as you're gluing it onto the face. Be sure you don't cut too shallow either, or the teeth will look super bulky. Once you have teeth you like, use fabric glue (I use Unique Stitch) or even Tacky Glue to cover the back of the teeth. Then place the teeth on your monster's face (after stuffing) and use a heavy book to weigh them down as they dry.

basic bowling-pin body

Lil' Love Slug

Who says slugs can't be cute? This one proves just how adorable and "snuggle-able" slugs can be! How cute would it be to tuck one of these guys into your next bouquet of "Get Well Soon" flowers?

SAMPLE

Rios from Malabrigo (100% pure merino superwash; 100 g; 210 yds) in color 37 Lettuce (4)

About 6" tall, from head to base

MATERIALS

Approx 18 g (38 yds) of worsted-weight yarn (4)

US size 5 (3.75 mm) needles

1 pair of 12 mm safety eyes

Small amount of waste yarn

BODY

Work body following instructions for Basic Bowling-Pin Body (page 29) through rnd 36.

Rnd 37: (Ssk, K12, K2tog) twice. (28 sts)

Rnd 38: Knit all sts.

Rnd 39: K4, place next 20 sts on waste yarn, K4 across gap to end of rnd; 8 sts rem on your needles to work first eye stem.

LEFT EYE STEM

Rnd 1: K1f&b, knit to last st, K1f&b. (10 sts)

Rnd 2: Knit all sts.

Rnd 3: (K1f&b, K4) twice. (12 sts)

Rnds 4–8: Knit all sts.

Rnd 9: K2tog around. (6 sts)

Add safety eye and stuff eye stem. Cut yarn and use tapestry needle to thread tail through rem sts to close eye stem.

Move first 6 sts and last 6 sts on waste yarn onto your needles. Join yarn and use Kitchener st to graft these 12 sts closed.

RIGHT EYE STEM

Rnd 1: Sl rem 8 sts on waste yarn to your needle. Be sure beg of rnd is in center near last grafted sts. Join yarn and knit all sts.

Rnd 2: K3, K1f&b in next 2 sts, knit to end of rnd. (10 sts)

Rnd 3: Knit all sts.

Rnd 4: (K1f&b, K4) twice. (12 sts)

Rnds 5–9: Knit all sts.

Rnd 10: K2tog around. (6 sts)

Again, add safety eye and a bit of stuffing to the eye stem. Cut yarn and use tapestry needle to thread tail through rem sts to close eye stem.

BASE

Work base following instructions for "Basic Bowling-Pin-Body Base" (page 30). Be sure to stuff slug before closing base. Cut yarn and use tapestry needle to thread tail through rem sts to close base.

basic bowling-pin body

Flyspeck Fox

Woodland critters seem to have grown very popular in the last few years, and this cutie-pie is a perfect example of why! I decided to keep him simple without arms or legs, but he would be just as darling with the Runty Raccoon (page 31) arms and legs. If you add limbs, don't forget to give him white paws!

SAMPLE

A Shepherd Worsted from Lorna's Laces (100% superwash merino wool; 4 oz; 225 yds) in color 38ns Brick (4)

B Shepherd Worsted from Lorna's Laces in color 0ns Natural

About 6" tall, from ears to base

MATERIALS

Using worsted-weight yarn, (4)

A Approx 18 g (36 yds)

B Approx 5 g (11 yds)

Waste yarn in a color different than A

US size 5 (3.75 mm) needles

1 pair of 9 mm safety eyes

15 mm safety nose

BODY

Using A and following instructions for Basic Bowling-Pin Body (page 29), CO and work as follows.

Rnds 1–28: Work as written.

Rnd 29: K4, switch to waste yarn and knit next 6 sts in waste yarn. Sl these 6 sts back to your LH needle purlwise; using working yarn, knit across waste yarn sts and to end of rnd. This rnd will become fox's nose.

Rnd 30 to end of body: Work as written.

NOSE

Work nose before base to allow access to attach safety nose.

Release 12 held sts by slipping 6 top and 6 bottom sts to your needle tips and removing waste yarn. (See "Where to Go for Help" on page 14.)

Rnd 1: Using B, (K6, PU 1 st from gap between top and bottom) twice. (14 sts)

Rnds 2 and 3: Knit all sts.

Rnd 4: (Ssk, K3, K2tog) twice. (10 sts)

Rnds 5 and 6: Knit all sts.

Rnd 7: (Ssk, K1, K2tog) twice. (6 sts)

Stuff nose. Cut yarn and use tapestry needle to thread tail through rem sts to close nose. Attach safety eyes and nose and beg to stuff head.

BASE

Be sure you have knit nose and attached safety eyes and nose prior to knitting base. Using B, work fox body base following instructions for "Basic Bowling-Pin-Body Base" (page 30).

EAR

Make 2.

Rnd 1: Using A and circular needle for Magic Loop method, pick up 5 and 5 sts (see page 11) from one side of top of head.

Rnds 2–4: Knit all sts.

Rnd 5: Switch to B and knit all sts. You'll cont in B to end of ear.

Rnd 6: (Ssk, K1, K2tog) twice. (6 sts)

Rnd 7: Knit all sts.

Cut yarn and use tapestry needle to thread tail through rem sts to close ear.

TAIL

Rnd 1: Using A and circular needle for Magic Loop method, pick up 5 and 5 sts from bottom center of back of body.

Rnds 2 and 3: Knit all sts.

Rnd 4: (K1f&b, K3, K1f&b) twice. (14 sts)

Rnds 5 and 6: Knit all sts.

Rnd 7: (K1f&b, K5, K1f&b) twice. (18 sts)

Rnds 8–21: Knit all sts, changing to B on rnd 20, and cont for remainder of tail.

Rnd 22: K2tog around. (9 sts)

Rnd 23: Knit all sts.

Rnd 24: K2tog around, ending K1. (5 sts)

Stuff tail. Cut yarn and use tapestry needle to thread tail through rem sts to close tail.

Bantam Bunny

I know; critters in clothes? I couldn't help myself. Adding a sweater is a great way to make a small amount of yardage go even further, since it lessens how much of your main color you'll need and the sweater itself takes almost no yarn.

SAMPLE

A Shepherd Worsted from Lorna's Laces (100% superwash merino wool; 4 oz; 225 yds) in color 211 Monkeyshines (4)

B Shepherd Worsted from Lorna's Laces in color 13ns Aqua

C Shepherd Worsted from Lorna's Laces in color 0ns Natural

About 8" tall, from head to toe

MATERIALS

Using worsted-weight yarn, (4)

A Approx 20 g (42 yds)

B Approx 7 g (15 yds)

C Approx 6 g (13 yds)

US size 5 (3.75 mm) needles

1 pair of 9 mm safety eyes

15 mm safety nose

BODY

Following instructions for Basic Bowling-Pin Body (page 29), CO with B and work as follows.

Rnd 1: With B.

Rnds 2–23: 1 rnd C, 1 rnd B (ending in B).

Rnd 24 to end of body: With A.

LEG

Make 2.

Rnd 1: Using A and circular needle for Magic Loop method, from bottom edge of body, pick up 4 sts from front CO edge and 4 sts from back CO edge (see page 11).

Rnds 2 and 3: Knit all sts.

Rnd 4: (K1f&b, K3) twice. (10 sts)

Rnds 5 and 6: Knit all sts.

Rnd 7: (K4, K1f&b) twice. (12 sts)

Rnds 8 and 9: Knit all sts.

Rnd 10: (K1f&b, K5) twice. (14 sts)

Rnds 11 and 12: Knit all sts.

Rnd 13: (K6, K1f&b) twice. (16 sts)

Rnds 14–23: Knit all sts.

Rnd 24: K2tog around. (8 sts)

Stuff leg. Cut yarn and use tapestry needle to thread tail through rem sts to close leg. Once legs have been stuffed, stuff body and add eyes and nose, then whipstitch base closed between legs.

ARM

Make 2.

Rnds 1–18 are worked in stripe patt: 1 rnd B, 1 rnd C.

Rnd 1: Using B and circular needle for Magic Loop method, pick up 3 sts from neck dec rnd and 3 sts from 1 rnd below.

Rnds 2 and 3: Knit all sts.

Rnd 4: (K1f&b, K2) twice. (8 sts)

Rnds 5 and 6: Knit all sts.

Rnd 7: (K3, K1f&b) twice. (10 sts)

Rnds 8 and 9: Knit all sts.

Rnd 10: (K1f&b, K4) twice. (12 sts)

Rnds 11 and 12: Knit all sts.

Rnd 13: (K5, K1f&b) twice. (14 sts)

Rnds 14–24: Knit all sts. Switch to A on rnd 19 and cont with A to end of arm.

Rnd 25: K2tog around. (7 sts)

Stuff hand. Cut yarn and use tapestry needle to thread tail through rem sts to close hand.

EAR

Make 2.

I picked up ear sts from front to back to create a more lop-eared-looking bunny. These ears would also look excellent picked up from the center of the head to the side.

Rnd 1: Using A and circular needle for Magic Loop method, pick up 3 and 3 sts from one side of top of head.

Rnd 2: Knit all sts.

Rnd 3: (K1f&b, K2) twice. (8 sts)

Rnd 4: Knit all sts.

Rnd 5: (K3, K1f&b) twice. (10 sts)

Rnd 6: Knit all sts.

Rnd 7: (K1f&b, K4) twice. (12 sts)

Rnd 8: Knit all sts.

Rnd 9: (K5, K1f&b) twice. (14 sts)

Rnds 10–24: Knit all sts.

Rnd 25: (Ssk, K3, K2tog) twice. (10 sts)

Rnds 26 and 27: Knit all sts.

Rnd 28: (Ssk, K1, K2tog) twice. (6 sts)

Rnd 29: Knit all sts.

Cut yarn and use tapestry needle to thread tail through rem sts to close ear.

TAIL

Rnd 1: Using C and circular needle for Magic Loop method, pick up 4 and 4 sts from bottom center of back of body.

Rnd 2: K1f&b all sts. (16 sts)

Rnd 3: Knit all sts.

Rnd 4: (K1f&b, K1) around. (24 sts)

Rnds 5–8: Knit all sts.

Rnd 9: (K2tog, K1) around. (16 sts)

Rnd 10: Knit all sts.

Rnd 11: K2tog around. (8 sts)

Stuff tail. Cut yarn and use tapestry needle to thread tail through rem sts to close tail.

Basic Uni-Body

The first knitting pattern I ever wrote was for a body shape like this where the legs and the body were all one piece. I love the look of this—nice and clean and simple—and it can be turned into about a million different creatures.

For this design, I gave the body a disproportionately large head to play up the cuteness of the face and the tinyness of the body. Because the legs and the body are knit all as one piece, this guy is a quick knit and doesn't use much yarn. I hope my variations, everything from a monkey to a ninja, serve as a good jumping-off point for you to create your very own uni-body creatures!

BASIC UNI-BODY SAMPLE

Rios from Malabrigo (100% pure merino superwash; 100 g; 210 yds) in color 128 Fresco y Seco (4)

Approx 5½" tall, from head to toe

MATERIALS

Approx 23 g (50 yds) of worsted-weight yarn (4)

40" circular needle 2 or 3 sizes smaller than that recommended for your yarn (for Magic Loop method)

US size 5 (3.75 mm) needles

1 pair of 12 mm safety eyes

BASIC UNI-BODY LEGS AND BODY

Cast on 6 sts per leg and set yourself up to beg working in the round using Magic Loop method (see "Two-at-a-Time Legs" on page 12).

Rnd 1: K1f&b around. (12 sts per leg for 24 sts total)

Rnds 2–11: Knit all sts.

Rnd 12: K6 of first leg. Turn your work so you're looking at WS of leg and use knit CO (page 79) to CO 6 sts. Turn your work back to RS, and using yarn from leg 1, knit across all 12 sts of leg 2. Cont in yarn from leg 1, turn your work once again so that WS is facing you. Use knit CO to CO 6 sts. Turn work once again and cont with yarn from leg 1, knit final 6 sts of leg 1 (36 sts). Cut yarn from leg 2. You'll stuff and add safety eyes later through hole created here with additional CO sts.

Beg body.

Rnds 1–15: Knit all sts.

Rnd 16: (K2tog, K1) around. (24 sts)

Rnd 17: Knit all sts.

Rnd 18: (K1f&b, K1) around. (36 sts)

Rnd 19: Knit all sts.

Rnd 20: (K1f&b, K7, K1f&b, K8, K1f&b) twice. (42 sts)

Rnds 21–28: Knit all sts.

Rnd 29: (K2tog, K5) around. (36 sts)

Rnd 30: Knit all sts.

Rnd 31: (K2tog, K2) around. (27 sts)

Rnd 32: Knit all sts.

Rnd 33: (K2tog, K1) around. (18 sts)

Rnd 34: Knit all sts.

Rnd 35: K2tog around. (9 sts)

Cut yarn and use tapestry needle to thread tail through rem sts to close head.

BASIC UNI-BODY ARM

Make 2.

Rnd 1: Using circular needle for Magic Loop method, pick up 4 sts from neck dec rnd and 4 sts from 1 rnd below (see page 11).

Rnds 2–15: Knit all sts.

Rnd 16: (K1f&b, K2, K1f&b) twice. (12 sts)

Rnds 17–21: Knit all sts.

Rnd 22: K2tog around. (6 sts)

Stuff hand. Cut yarn and use tapestry needle to thread tail through rem sts to close hand.

Small Squirrel

There was a squirrel at my house that used to run up and down a tree less than a foot outside of my fenced yard. This squirrel was the bane of my pugs' existence. He'd torment them at great lengths. When we moved, I was happy to leave the squirrel behind but sure enough, at our new house there was a new squirrel ready and waiting for more pug taunting to begin. I plan to make my pugs one of these squirrels (minus safety eyes and nose, of course!) so that they can take out their frustrations on him!

basic uni-body

SAMPLE

A Merino 5 from Crystal Palace Yarns (100% superwash merino wool; 50 g; 110 yds) in color 1008 Old Gold (4)

B Splash from Crystal Palace Yarns (100% polyester; 85 g; 100 yds) in color 7183 Lioness (6)

Approx 6" tall, from ears to toes

MATERIALS

A Approx 22 g (49 yds) of worsted-weight yarn (4)

B Approx 13 g (16 yds) of novelty yarn (6)

US size 5 (3.75 mm) needles

1 pair of 9 mm safety eyes

15 mm safety nose

BODY

Using A and following instructions for "Basic Uni-Body Legs and Body" (page 41), CO 6 sts for each leg and work as written.

ARM

Make 2.

Rnd 1: Using A and circular needle for Magic Loop method, pick up 4 sts from dec rnd and 4 sts from 1 rnd below.

Rnds 2 and 3: Knit all sts.

Rnd 4: (K1f&b, K3) twice. (10 sts)

Rnds 5 and 6: Knit all sts.

Rnd 7: (K4, K1f&b) twice. (12 sts)

Rnds 8–19: Knit all sts.

Rnd 20: K2tog around. (6 sts)

Stuff arm. Cut yarn and use tapestry needle to thread tail through rem sts to close arm.

EAR

Make 2.

Rnd 1: Using A and circular needle for Magic Loop method, pick up 2 and 2 sts from one side of top of head.

Rnd 2: (K1f&b, K1) twice. (6 sts)

Rnd 3: Knit all sts.

Rnd 4: (K1f&b, K2) twice. (8 sts)

Rnds 5–7: Knit all sts.

Cut yarn and use tapestry needle to thread tail through rem sts to close ear.

TAIL

Rnd 1: Using B and circular needle for Magic Loop method, pick up 5 and 5 sts horizontally across *backside* of body.

Rnds 2 and 3: Knit all sts.

Rnd 4: (K1f&b, K4) twice. (12 sts)

Rnds 5 and 6: Knit all sts.

Rnd 7: (K5, K1f&b) twice. (14 sts)

Rnds 8–19: Knit all sts.

Rnd 20: K2tog around. (7 sts)

Stuff tail. Cut yarn and use tapestry needle to thread tail through rem sts to close tail.

Nano Ninja

I already loved ninjas, but this guy is so tiny and amazing that I think he has made me love ninjas even more! I made one of these guys for my son and the ninja hides all around our house, popping out when you least expect him. We call him the "Cookie-Ninja" since he is always on the hunt for cookies.

SAMPLE

A Shepherd Worsted from Lorna's Laces (100% superwash merino wool; 4 oz; 225 yds) in color 58ns Kerfuffle (4)

B Shepherd Worsted from Lorna's Laces in color 0ns Natural

About 6" tall, from head to toe

MATERIALS

Using worsted-weight yarn, (4)

A Approx 23 g (46 yds)

B Approx 2 g (4 yds)

US size 5 (3.75 mm) needles

1 pair of 9 mm safety eyes

BODY

Using A and following instructions for "Basic Uni-Body Legs and Body" (page 41), CO 6 sts for each leg and work as follows.

Rnds 1–22: With A.

Rnds 23–26: K6 with A, K9 with B, knit to end of rnd with A.

Rnd 27 to end of body: With A.

ARMS

Make 2.

Using A, follow instructions for "Basic Uni-Body Arm" (page 42).

TIES

Ties are knit flat (not in the round).

Make 2. Make bottom tie first.

Row 1: Using A, pick up 4 sts in a straight line above arm.

Rows 2 and 3: Knit all sts

Row 4: (K1f&b, K1) twice (6 sts)

Rows 5–8: Knit all sts

Cut yarn and use tapestry needle to thread tail through rem sts to close tie.

Rep rows 1–8 for top tie, picking up 4 sts immediately above bottom tie.

Compact Cat in Pajamas

This cat in pajamas is really the Cat's Pajamas! Tiny cats in clothes spike them right off the cuteness scale. This guy is so cuddly, how fun would he be for favors at a little girls' sleepover party?

SAMPLE

A Rios from Malabrigo (100% pure merino superwash; 100 g; 210 yds) in color 131 Sand Bank (4)

B Rios from Malabrigo in color 412 Teal Feather

C Rios from Malabrigo in color 139 Pocion

Approx 7" tall, from ears to toes

basic uni-body

MATERIALS

Using worsted-weight yarn, (**4**)

A Approx 14 g (30 yds)

B Approx 13 g (28 yds)

C Approx 13 g (28 yds)

US size 5 (3.75 mm) needles

1 pair of 9 mm safety eyes

15 mm safety nose

LEGS AND BODY

Using A and following instructions for "Basic Uni-Body Legs and Body" (page 41), CO 6 sts for each leg and work as follows.

Rnds 1–4: With A.

Rnds 5–17: Switch to B and knit all sts.

Rnd 18: K6 of first leg. Turn your work so you're looking at WS of leg and use knit CO (page 79) to CO 6 sts. Turn your work back to RS, and using yarn from leg 1, knit across all 12 sts of leg 2. Cont in yarn from leg 1, turn your work once again so that WS is facing you. Use knit CO to CO 6 sts. Turn work and cont with yarn from leg 1, knit final 6 sts of leg 1 (36 sts). Cut yarn from leg 2. You'll stuff and add safety eyes later through hole created here with additional CO sts.

Beg body.

Rnds 1–15: Knit all sts with B.

Rnd 16: Switch to A, (K2tog, K1) around. (24 sts) You'll cont in A to end of head.

Rnd 17: Knit all sts.

Rnd 18: (K1f&b, K1) around. (36 sts)

Rnd 19: Knit all sts.

Rnd 20: (K1f&b, K7, K1f&b, K8, K1f&b) twice. (42 sts)

Rnds 21–28: Knit all sts.

Rnd 29: (K2tog, K5) around. (36 sts)

Rnd 30: Knit all sts.

Rnd 31: (K2tog, K2) around. (27 sts)

Rnd 32: Knit all sts.

Rnd 33: (K2tog, K1) around. (18 sts)

Rnd 34: Knit all sts.

Rnd 35: K2tog around. (9 sts)

Cut yarn and use tapestry needle to thread tail through rem sts to close head.

ARM

Make 2.

Rnd 1: Using B and circular needle for Magic Loop method, pick up 5 sts from neck dec rnd and 5 sts from 1 rnd below.

Rnds 2–20: Knit all sts in B.

Rnds 21–26: Knit all sts in A.

Rnd 27: K2tog around. (5 sts)

Stuff hand. Cut yarn and use tapestry needle to thread tail through rem sts to close hand.

EAR

Make 2.

Rnd 1: Using A and circular needle for Magic Loop method, pick up 5 and 5 sts (see page 11) from one side of top of head.

Rnds 2 and 3: Knit all sts.

Rnd 4: (Ssk, K3) twice. (8 sts)

Rnd 5: Knit all sts.

Rnd 6: (K2, K2tog) twice. (6 sts)

Cut yarn and use tapestry needle to thread tail through rem sts to close ear.

TAIL

Rnd 1: Using A and circular needle for Magic Loop method, pick up 4 and 4 sts across *backside* of body.

Rnds 2–33: Knit all sts.

Cut yarn and use tapestry needle to thread tail through rem sts to close tail.

BLANKET

Blanket is knit flat (not in the round).

With C, and your choice of needles, CO 28 sts. DO NOT JOIN.

Rows 1, 3, 5, 8, 10, and 12: (K4, P4) to last 4 sts, K4.

Rows 2, 4, 9, and 11: (P4, K4) to last 4 sts, P4.

Rows 6, 7, 13, and 14: Knit all sts.

Rep these 14 rows one more time.

Work rows 1–11 once more.

Loosely BO all sts in patt.

Blanket from Gauge Swatch

If you made a gauge swatch before knitting the cat, you can use that square for the Compact Cat in Pajamas' blanket!

Meager Mouse

Although this guy uses more than 50 yards, I decided it was okay since he is so cute. Look at those giant ears! If you have less gray yarn, just give this guy a sweater to cut down on how much yardage you need.

SAMPLE

Merino Worsted from Another Crafty Girl (100% superwash merino; 100 g; 215 yds) in color Foil (4)

Approx 7½" tall, from ears to toes

MATERIALS

Approx 30 g (65 yds)* of worsted-weight yarn (4)

US size 5 (3.75 mm) needles

1 pair of 9 mm safety eyes

15 mm safety nose

This one uses a little more yarn than other projects in this book. Give him a stripey sweater if you think you'll run short.

LEGS AND BODY

Following instructions for "Basic Uni-Body Legs and Body" (page 41), CO 6 sts for each leg and work as written.

ARM

Make 2.

Following instructions for "Basic Uni-Body Arm" (page 42), CO and work as follows.

Rnds 1–21: As written.

Rnds 22–24: Knit all sts.

Rnd 25: K2tog around. (6 sts)

Stuff hand. Cut yarn and use tapestry needle to thread tail through rem sts to close hand.

EAR

Make 2.

Rnd 1: Using circular needle for Magic Loop method, pick up 8 and 8 sts (see page 11) from top and side of head.

Rnd 2: (K1f&b, K6, K1f&b) twice. (20 sts)

Rnd 3: Knit all sts.

Rnd 4: (K1f&b, K8, K1f&b) twice. (24 sts)

Rnds 5–10: Knit all sts.

Rnd 11: (Ssk, K8, K2tog) twice. (20 sts)

Rnd 12: (Ssk, K6, K2tog) twice. (16 sts)

Rnd 13: (Ssk, K4, K2tog) twice. (12 sts)

Rnd 14: (Ssk, K2, K2tog) twice. (8 sts)

Cut yarn and use tapestry needle to thread tail through rem sts to close ear.

TAIL

Rnd 1: Using circular needle for Magic Loop method, pick up 3 and 3 sts across *backside* of body.

Rnds 2–30: Knit all sts.

Cut yarn and use tapestry needle to thread tail through rem sts to close tail.

Micro Monkey

Who doesn't love a monkey? I see monkeys on everything these days. I am sure you'll find uses for a whole barrel full of micro monkeys!

SAMPLE

A Shepherd Worsted from Lorna's Laces (100% superwash merino wool; 4 oz [4] 5 yds) in color 36ns Chocolate

B Shepherd Worsted from Lorna's Laces in color 15ns Chino

About 6" tall, from head to toe

MATERIALS

A Approx 21 g (42 yds)

B Approx 5 g (10 yds)

US size 5 (3.75 mm) needles

1 pair of 9 mm safety eyes

LEGS AND BODY

Using B and following instructions for "Basic Uni-Body Legs and Body" (page 41), CO 6 sts for each leg and work as follows.

Rnds 1–5: With B.

Rnd 6 to end of body: With A.

ARM

Make 2.

Rnd 1: Using A and circular needle for Magic Loop method, pick up 4 sts from neck dec rnd and 4 sts from 1 rnd below (see page 11).

Rnds 2–20: Knit all sts.

Rnd 21: Switch to B and (K1f&b, K2, K1f&b) twice (12 sts). Work in B to end of hand.

Rnds 22–28: Knit all sts.

Stuff hand. Cut yarn and use tapestry needle to thread tail through rem sts to close hand.

TAIL

Rnd 1: Using A and circular needle for Magic Loop method, pick up 3 and 3 sts from bottom center of back of body.

Rnds 2–30: Knit all sts.

Cut yarn and use tapestry needle to thread tail through rem sts to close tail.

EAR

Make 2.

Rnd 1: Using B and circular needle for Magic Loop method, pick up 3 and 3 sts from lower side of head.

Rnd 2: (K1f&b, K1, K1f&b) twice. (10 sts)

Rnds 3–7: Knit all sts.

Cut yarn and use tapestry needle to thread tail through rem sts to close ear.

NOSE

Rnd 1: Using B and circular needle for Magic Loop method, pick up 20 sts from center of face as follows: Pick up 8 sts in a straight line, then pick up 1 st over and up 1 rnd from last st picked up, then pick up 1 st above that. Pick up 8 more sts 2 rnds above first 2 picked up, then pick up 1 st over and down 1 rnd and 1 st, then pick up 1 st in the rnd below. (20 sts)

Rnds 2–5: Knit all sts.

Rnd 6: K2tog around. (10 sts)

Embroider 2 little lines for monkey's nostrils and stuff nose. Then cut yarn and use tapestry needle to thread tail through rem sts to close nose.

Little Luchador

Oh my goodness, I love Lucha Libre (professional wrestling in Mexico, where they wear colorful masks)! As soon as I created this body shape, I knew it was perfectly suited to turn into a little wrestler. To make it more fun, make two so that you can have little wrestling matches. Err, I mean your kids can have mini Lucha Libre matches. Yeah, your kids. That's what I meant . . . .

SAMPLE

A Shepherd Worsted from Lorna's Laces (100% superwash merino wool; 4 oz; 225 yds) in color 15ns Chino (4)

B Greater Poison from The Wool Dispensary (100% superwash merino wool; 107 g; 180 yds) in color Badass Unicorn (4)

C Scrap of white worsted-weight yarn

About 6" tall, from head to toe

MATERIALS

Using worsted-weight yarn, (4)

A Approx 17 g (34 yds)

B Approx 21 g (38 yds)

C Approx 1 g (2 yds)

US size 5 (3.75 mm) needles

1 pair of 9 mm safety eyes

LEGS AND BODY

Following instructions for "Basic Uni-Body Legs and Body" (page 41), CO 6 sts with A for each leg and work as follows.

basic uni-body

Rnds 1–11 of legs: With A.

Rnd 12 of legs: With B.

Rnds 1–7 of body: With B.

Rnds 8–16: With A.

Rnds 17–20: With B.

Rnds 21 and 22: K5 with B, K11 with C, knit to end of rnd with B.

Rnds 23 and 24: With B.

Rnds 25–28: K6 with B, K9 with A, knit to end of rnd with B.

Rnd 29 to end of body: With B.

ARM

Make 2.

Rnd 1: Using A and circular needle for Magic Loop method, pick up 5 sts from neck dec rnd and 5 sts from 1 rnd below (see page 11).

Rnds 2–12: Knit all sts.

Rnd 13: Switch to B and K1f&b around (20 sts). You'll cont in B to end of hand.

Rnds 14–20: Knit all sts.

Rnd 21: K2tog around. (10 sts)

Stuff hand. Cut yarn and use tapestry needle to thread tail through rem sts to close hand.

CAPE

Using B and 2 dpns, use I-cord CO to CO 12 sts as follows.

CO 3 sts onto 1 dpn. Slide these 3 sts to RH side of your dpn, positioning working yarn behind last st on needle and setting yourself up to knit an I-cord.

K1f&b in first st, knit next 2 sts. You now have 4 sts on RH needle.

Sl first 3 sts knitwise from RH needle to LH needle, K1f&b in first st on LH needle, then K2 as before. You'll now have 5 sts on RH needle.

Sl first 3 sts knitwise from RH needle to LH needle once more, K1f&b, K2 once again. Cont to sl first 3 sts knitwise from RH needle to LH needle and K1f&b, K2 until you have 14 sts on RH needle (12 original plus 2 extra sts).

Sl first 3 sts knitwise from RH needle to LH needle, K2tog, K1.

Sl first 2 sts knitwise from RH needle to LH needle, K2tog. Your I-cord CO is done, with 12 sts on needle.

Set up row: (K1, P1) across.

Row 1: K1f&b, (K1, P1) to last st, K1f&b.

Row 2: (P1, K1) across.

Row 3: (K1, P1) across.

Row 4: (P1, K1) across.

Row 5: K1f&b, (P1, K1) to last st, K1f&b.

Row 6: (K1, P1) across.

Row 7: (P1, K1) across.

Row 8: (K1, P1) across.

Rep rows 1–8 three more times. You'll have 24 sts at end of 4th rep. Then rep rows 7 and 8 once more (or until desired length). Loosely BO all sts in patt.

CAPE TIE

Make 2.

Rnd 1: Using B and 1 dpn, PU 2 sts from one end of I-cord CO.

Rnds 2–30: Knit all sts as an I-cord (see "Abbreviations and Glossary" on page 79) or until tie is long enough to tie cape around wrestler's neck. Cut yarn and use tapestry needle to thread tail through rem sts to close tie.

Basic Biscuit Body

I named this one the Basic Biscuit Body because the shape reminds me of a Milano cookie. I love that this body seems to have no beginning or end. This one was really fun to turn sideways and lengthwise and always come out with a good-looking critter. And it includes a knitting technique I am totally in love with—the Turkish cast on. It almost seems like the Turkish cast on was designed just to make this shape possible. If you haven't tried this technique before, I encourage you to learn a new, surprisingly easy technique. I even made sure to include a video online to help you get going. See "Where to Go for Help" on page 14.

I hope this shape inspires you to come up with all kinds of biscuity-shaped creations, or at least go eat some biscuits!

BASIC BISCUIT-BODY SAMPLE

Superwash Worsted from SweetGeorgia Yarns (100% superwash merino wool; 115 g; 200 yds) in Snapdragon 4

Approx 8½" tall

MATERIALS

Approx 23 g (50 yds) of worsted-weight yarn 4

40" circular needle 2 or 3 sizes smaller than that recommended for your yarn (for Magic Loop method)

US size 5 (3.75 mm) needles

1 pair of 12 mm safety eyes

BASIC BISCUIT BODY

Use circular needle for Magic Loop method and Turkish CO to CO 20 sts (10 loops per needle). As you start rnd 1, join for working in the round, making sure not to twist sts. PM to indicate beg of rnd.

Rnd 1: Knit all sts.

Rnd 2: (K1f&b, K8, K1f&b) twice. (24 sts)

Rnd 3: Knit all sts.

Rnd 4: (K1f&b, K10, K1f&b) twice. (28 sts)

Rnd 5: Knit all sts.

Rnd 6: (K1f&b, K12, K1f&b) twice. (32 sts)

Rnds 7–34: Knit all sts.

Rnd 35: (Ssk, K12, K2tog) twice. (28 sts)

Rnd 36: Knit all sts.

Rnd 37: (Ssk, K10, K2tog) twice. (24 sts)

Rnd 38: Knit all sts.

Rnd 39: (Ssk, K8, K2tog) twice. (20 sts)

Add any eyes, patches, etc. that need tying off or securing inside body now. Stuff body. Cut yarn leaving a long tail and use tapestry needle to work Kitchener st to close sts.

BASIC BISCUIT-BODY ARM

Make 2.

Rnd 1: Using circular needle for Magic Loop method, pick up 3 sts from neck dec rnd and 3 sts from 1 rnd below (see page 11).

Rnds 2–20: Knit all sts.

Rnd 21: (K1f&b, K1, K1f&b) twice. (10 sts)

Rnds 22–26: Knit all sts.

Rnd 27: K2tog around. (5 sts)

Stuff hand. Cut yarn and use tapestry needle to thread tail through rem sts to close hand.

BASIC BISCUIT-BODY LEG

Make 2.

Rnd 1: Using circular needle for Magic Loop method, pick up 3 and 3 sts from bottom of body. For both legs, be sure that beg of rnd is on *backside* of body.

Rnds 2–20: Knit all sts.

Working just first 3 sts of rnd and holding last 3 sts of rnd on your cable, work back and forth as follows.

Row 1: Sl 1, knit to end. Turn.

Row 2: Sl 1, purl to end. Turn.

Work rows 1 and 2 for a total of 4 rows, ending on a purl row.

Rnd 1 of foot: Turn work so you're ready to knit. PM to indicate new beg of rnd. Knit across heel sts once more. Using same needle tip, PU 2 sts from LH side of heel flap. Flip to other needle tip and knit across held instep sts and PU 2 sts from RH side of heel flap. (10 sts)

Rnd 2: K3, K2tog, K3, ssk. (8 sts)

Rnds 3–9: Knit all sts.

Stuff foot. Cut yarn and use tapestry needle to thread tail through rem sts to close foot.

Peter Bunyan (Paul's Tiny Lumberjack Cousin)

Though I started into this design focused on creating a lumberjack, I can't help but see this guy as a fisherman as well. Maybe because my dad

is a fisherman and this tiny guy actually looks just like him. Whichever you see, lumberjack or fisherman, you can make him a tiny sidekick: Snack-Sized Yak (page 20) in blue for a lumberjack, or Fractional Fish (page 58) for a fisherman!

SAMPLE

Remix from Berroco (30% nylon, 27% cotton, 24% acrylic, 10% silk, 9% linen; 100 g/3.5 oz; 216 yds/200 m) (4) in the following colors:

A 3949 Nightfall

B 3992 Sumac

C 3903 Almond

D 3967 Bittersweet

E 3990 Cocoa

Approx 10" tall, from head to toe

MATERIALS

Using worsted-weight yarn, (4)

A Approx 9 g (20 yds) (dark blue)

B Approx 8 g (18 yds) (rust)

C Approx 5 g (11 yds) (beige)

D Approx 9 g (20 yds) (charcoal)

E Approx 4 g (9 yds) (brown)

US size 5 (3.75 mm) needles

1 pair of 9 mm safety eyes

BODY

Following instructions for Basic Biscuit Body (page 51), CO with A and work as follows.

Rnds 1–14: With A.

Rnds 15–28: With B.

Rnd 29 to end of body: With C.

Once finished with the body, cut 7 pieces of brown yarn 6" long and make fringe across the top of the head for hair (see "Making Fringe" on page 24). Starting in the middle, I put fringe on 7 spots for the hair. Once you're happy with the hair placement, trim the fringe very short (½" or shorter).

ARM

Make 2.

Rnd 1: Using B and circular needle for Magic Loop method, pick up 4 sts from shirt line of body and 4 sts from 1 rnd below (see page 11).

Rnds 2–22: Knit all sts in B.

Rnds 23–30: Switch to C and knit all sts. Cont in C to end of hand.

Stuff hand. Cut yarn and use tapestry needle to thread tail through rem sts to close hand.

LEG

Make 2.

Rnd 1: Using A and circular needle for Magic Loop method, pick up 5 sts from bottom and 5 sts from increase edge of base of body. For both legs, be sure that beg of rnd is on *backside* of body.

Rnds 2–18: With A, knit all sts.

Rnds 19–28: Switch to D and knit all sts. Cont in D to end of foot.

Working just first 5 sts of rnd and holding last 5 sts of rnd on cable, work back and forth as follows.

Row 1: Sl 1, knit to end. Turn.

Row 2: Sl 1, purl to end. Turn.

Work rows 1 and 2 for a total of 6 rows, ending on a purl row.

Rnd 1 of foot: Turn your work so you're ready to knit. PM to indicate new beg of rnd. Knit across heel sts once more. Using same needle tip, PU 4 sts from LH side of heel flap (3 gusset sts plus 1 st in gap). Flip to other needle tip and knit across held instep sts and PU 4 sts from RH side of heel flap (3 gusset sts plus 1 st in gap). (18 sts)

Rnd 2: K5, K2tog, K2tog, K5, ssk, ssk. (14 sts)

Rnd 3: Knit all sts.

Rnd 4: K5, K2tog, K5, ssk. (12 sts)

Rnds 5–11: Knit all sts.

Rnd 12: K2tog around. (6 sts)

Stuff foot. Cut yarn and use tapestry needle to thread tail through rem sts to close foot.

SUSPENDER

Make 2.

Rnd 1: Using A and dpn to work as an I-cord (see page 79), pick up 3 sts in a line from pants line of body.

Rnds 2–24: Knit all rnds as an I-cord (or until suspender can cross in back to end at back pant line). Cut yarn and use tapestry needle to thread tail through rem sts to close suspender. Stitch end of suspender to back pants line.

HAT

Using D and circular needle for Magic Loop method, CO 32 sts and join for working in the rnd, making sure not to twist sts. PM to indicate beg of rnd.

Rnds 1–4: (K1, P1) around.

Rnds 5–13: Knit all sts.

Rnd 14: (K2tog, K2) around. (24 sts)

Rnd 15: Knit all sts.

Rnd 16: (K2tog, K1) around. (16 sts)

Rnd 17: Knit all sts.

Cut yarn and use tapestry needle to thread tail through rem sts to close hat. Weave in ends to finish hat.

BEARD

The beard is knit flat (not in the round). Using E, CO 5 sts.

Row 1: (K1, P1) across.

Row 2: K1f&b, P1, K1, P1, K1f&b. (7 sts)

Row 3: (P1, K1) across.

Row 4: K1f&b, (K1, P1) twice, K1, K1f&b. (9 sts)

Rows 5–10: (K1, P1) all sts.

Row 11: K1, P1, K1, BO next 3 sts, P1 K1. Middle 3 sts are BO. (6 sts)

Row 12: K1, P1, K1, use knit CO (see "Abbreviations and Glossary" on page 79) to CO 3 sts, K1, P1, K1. (9 sts)

Row 13: (K1, P1) all sts.

Row 14: K1, P2tog, sl1-K2tog-psso, P2tog, K1. (5 sts)

Row 15: Loosely BO all sts.

Sew beard to middle of face, with mouth end at top and longer side at bottom. Tack beard down on top edge so it's less rigid and more malleable, like a real beard—if a knitted mini beard can be realistic!

Not-Big Guinea Pig

This body shape cried out "Guinea Pig!" to me as I was creating it. I love how he looks with his tiny ears and arms. This guy would make the perfect present for the guinea-pig lover in your life. (We all know at least one guinea-pig lover, don't we?)

SAMPLE

A Remix from Berroco (30% nylon, 27% cotton, 24% acrylic, 10% silk, 9% linen; 100 g/3.5 oz; 216 yds/200 m) in color 3933 Patina 【4】

B Remix from Berroco in color 3901 Birch

Approx 6" tall, from head to toe

MATERIALS

Using worsted-weight yarn, 【4】

A Approx 13 g (28 yds)

B Approx 6 g (13 yds)

US size 5 (3.75 mm) needles

1 pair of 9 mm safety eyes

15 mm safety nose

BODY

Following instructions for Basic Biscuit Body (page 51), CO with A and work as follows.

Rnds 1–13: With A.

Rnds 14–26: With B.

Rnd 27: (K4 with A, K8 with B, K4 with A) twice.

Rnd 28: (K5 with A, K6 with B, K5 with A) twice.

Rnd 29: (K6 with A, K4 with B, K6 with A) twice.

Rnds 30–34: Rep rnd 29

Rnd 35 to end of body: With A.

Add eyes in face "patches" and nose between patches before stuffing and finishing body.

EAR

Make 2.

Rnd 1: Using A and circular needle for Magic Loop method, pick up 2 and 2 sts (see page 11) from *corner* of one side of top of head.

Rnd 2: (K1f&b, K1) twice. (6 sts)

Rnds 3 and 4: Knit all sts.

Cut yarn and use tapestry needle to thread tail through rem sts to close ear.

ARM

Make 2.

Rnd 1: Using A and circular needle for Magic Loop pick up 3 sts from right below eye patch and 3 sts from 1 rnd below.

Rnds 2 and 3: Knit all sts.

Rnd 4: (K1, K1f&b, K1) twice. (8 sts)

Rnds 5–9: Knit all sts.

Stuff hand. Cut yarn and use tapestry needle to thread tail through rem sts to close hand.

FOOT

Make 2.

Rnd 1: Using A and circular needle for Magic Loop pick up 3 and 3 sts from rounded sides of base of body.

Rnds 2 and 3: Knit all sts.

Rnd 4: (K1, K1f&b, K1) twice. (8 sts)

Rnds 5–10: Knit all sts.

Stuff foot. Cut yarn and use tapestry needle to thread tail through rem sts to close foot.

Half-Sized Hippo

I can't get over how cute this guy is! He was the first of this body shape I knit to lie down, and as soon as he was finished, I knew I was hooked on this orientation. With his little legs sticking out to the sides, doesn't he look like he is ready to swim if you were to drop him in water?

SAMPLE

Rios from Malabrigo (100% pure merino superwash; 100 g; 210 yds) in color 120 Lotus (4)

Approx 6" long, from head to toe

MATERIALS

Approx 19 g (28 yds) of worsted-weight yarn (4)

US size 5 (3.75 mm) needles

1 pair of 9 mm safety eyes

BODY

Work body following instructions for Basic Biscuit Body (page 51).

Embroider nostrils and attach safety eyes to CO end of hippo, then stuff body and finish as written.

When body is finished, add a tiny hippo tail by making fringe with 3 pieces of approx 8"-long yarn held together and centering it on non-eye end of body (see "Making Fringe" on page 24). Braid 3 pieces together and tie in a knot to finish tail, trimming to right length as needed.

EAR

Make 2.

Rnd 1: Using circular needle for Magic Loop method, pick up 2 and 2 sts (see page 11) from behind and to side of eye.

Rnd 2: (K1f&b, K1) twice. (6 sts)

Rnd 3: Knit all sts.

Rnd 4: (K1f&b, K2) twice. (8 sts)

Rnds 5 and 6: Knit all sts.

Cut yarn and use tapestry needle to thread tail through rem sts to close ear.

FRONT LEG

Make 2.

Rnd 1: Using circular needle for Magic Loop method, pick up 3 sts from same rnd as eyes and ears and 3 sts from one rnd below, but on sides of body.

Rnd 2: Knit all sts.

Rnd 3: (K1, K1f&b, K1) twice. (8 sts)

Rnd 4: Knit all sts.

Rnd 5: (K1, K1f&b, K2) twice. (10 sts)

Rnds 6–11: Knit all sts.

Rnd 12: K2tog around. (5 sts)

Stuff leg. Cut yarn and use tapestry needle to thread tail through rem sts to close foot.

BACK LEG

Make 2.

Work as for front leg, except pick up sts from rounded end of bottom of body.

basic biscuit body

Pithy Platypus

When I was little, my best friend absolutely loved platypuses, so they have always held a special place in my heart. If I had made this as a child, I am sure it would have been a treasured part of my friend's platypus collection!

SAMPLE

A Superwash Worsted from SweetGeorgia Yarns (100% superwash merino wool; 115 g; 200 yds) in color Bison 4

B Superwash Worsted from SweetGeorgia Yarns in color Charcoal

Approx 8½" long, from nose to tail

MATERIALS

Using worsted-weight yarn, 4

A Approx 17 g (31 yds)

B Approx 15 g (27 yds)

US size 5 (3.75 mm) needles

1 pair of 9 mm safety eyes

BODY

Using instructions for Basic Biscuit Body (page 51), CO with B and work as follows.

Rnds 1–15: With B.

Rnd 16 to end of body: With A.

Embroider nostrils in B section, and attach safety eyes 1 or 2 rnds beyond where A starts. Then stuff body and finish as written.

TAIL

Rnd 1: Using A and circular needle for Magic Loop method, pick up 6 and 6 sts (see page 11) from back end of body.

Rnds 2 and 3: Knit all sts.

Rnd 4: (K1f&b, K5) twice. (14 sts)

Rnds 5 and 6: Knit all sts.

Rnd 7: (K6, K1f&b) twice. (16 sts)

Rnds 8 and 9: Knit all sts.

Rnd 10: (K1f&b, K7) twice. (18 sts)

Rnds 11 and 12: Knit all sts.

Rnd 13: (K8, K1f&b) twice. (20 sts)

Rnds 14–24: Knit all sts.

Rnd 25: K2tog around. (10 sts)

Stuff tail. Cut yarn and use tapestry needle to thread tail through rem sts to close tail.

FOOT

Make 4.

Pick up sts for 2 front feet on same rnd as eyes but on sides. Pick up sts for 2 back feet on back rounded end by tail.

Rnd 1: Using circular needle for Magic Loop method, pick up 4 and 4 sts.

Rnd 2: K1f&b around. (16 sts)

Rnd 3: Knit all sts.

Rnd 4: (K1f&b, ssk, K1f&b twice, K2tog, K1f&b) twice. (20 sts)

Rnd 5: Knit all sts.

Rnd 6: (K2, ssk, K1f&b twice, K2tog, K2) twice.

Rnd 7: Knit all sts.

Stuff foot. Cut yarn leaving a long tail and use tapestry needle to work Kitchener st to close sts, adding more stuffing as needed.

Fractional Fish

I hope you'll want to create a whole school of these fishy friends! While creating this guy, all I could think of was making a fish mobile. For more ideas on a mobile, check out my "Bat Mobile" on page 75.

SAMPLE

A Rios from Malabrigo (100% pure merino superwash; 100 g; 210 yds) in color 16 Glazed Carrot

B Rios from Malabrigo in color 63 Natural

Approx 5½" long, from nose to tail.

MATERIALS

Using worsted-weight yarn, **4**

A Approx 9 g (19 yds)

B Approx 7 g (15 yds)

US size 5 (3.75 mm) needles

1 pair of 9 mm safety eyes

BODY

Following instructions for Basic Biscuit Body (page 51), CO with B and work as follows.

Rnds 1–12: With B, work as written.

Work remainder of body in 4 rnds A, 2 rnds B.

Rnds 13–29: Knit all sts. (32 sts)

Rnd 30: (Ssk, K12, K2tog) twice. (28 sts)

Rnd 31: Knit all sts.

Rnd 32: (Ssk, K10, K2tog) twice. (24 sts)

Rnd 33: Knit all sts.

Rnd 34: (Ssk, K8, K2tog) twice. (20 sts)

Add eyes to sides of body in 12 rnds of B before stuffing. Close body using Kitchener st.

TAIL

Rnd 1: Using A and circular needle for Magic Loop method, pick up 7 and 7 sts (see page 11) from back end of body on each side of Kitchener st seam.

Rnd 2: (K1f&b, K5, K1f&b) twice. (18 sts)

Rnds 3 and 4: Knit all sts.

Rnd 5: (K1f&b, K7, K1f&b) twice. (22 sts)

Rnds 6 and 7: Knit all sts.

Rnd 8: (K1f&b, K9, K1f&b) twice. (26 sts)

Rnds 9 and 10: Knit all sts.

Rnd 11: (K1f&b, K11, K1f&b) twice. (30 sts)

Rnd 12: Knit all sts.

Stuff tail. Cut yarn leaving a long tail and use tapestry needle to work Kitchener st to close sts, adding more stuffing as needed.

SIDE FIN

Make 2.

Rnd 1: Using A and circular needle for Magic Loop method, pick up 2 rows of 5 sts each, vertically, from first A stripe in body. Use photo above left or on page 59 for reference.

Rnds 2 and 3: Knit all sts.

Rnd 4: (Ssk, K3) twice. (8 sts)

Rnds 5 and 6: Knit all sts.

Rnd 7: (K2, K2tog) twice. (6 sts)

Cut yarn and use tapestry needle to thread tail through rem sts to close fin.

DORSAL (TOP) FIN

Rnd 1: Using A and circular needle for Magic Loop method, pick up 2 rows of 12 sts each, down the center top of fish. Use photo below or on page 58 for reference. Be sure that beg of rnd starts toward tail end of fish.

Rnd 2: Knit all sts.

Rnd 3: K10, K2tog, ssk, knit to end. (22 sts)

Rnd 4: K1f&b, K8, K2tog, ssk, knit to last st, K1f&b. (22 sts)

Rnd 5: K9, K2tog, ssk, K9. (20 sts)

Rnd 6: K8, K2tog, ssk, K8. (18 sts)

Rnd 7: K1f&b, K6, K2tog, ssk, knit to last st, K1f&b. (18 sts)

Rnd 8: K7, K2tog, ssk, K7. (16 sts)

Rnd 9: K6, K2tog, ssk, K6. (14 sts)

Rnd 10: K5, K2tog, ssk, K5. (12 sts)

Rnd 11: K4, K2tog, ssk, K4. (10 sts)

Cut yarn and use tapestry needle to thread tail through rem sts to close fin.

Undersized Unicorn

I love knitted mythical creatures, as if that wasn't quite obvious with the generous helping in this book. Inspired by the Wool Dispensary yarn color, Badass Unicorn, I knew I needed to create a unicorn featuring it. This one does the trick!

SAMPLE

A Shepherd Worsted from Lorna's Laces (100% superwash merino wool; 4 oz; 225 yds) in color Ons Natural (4)

B Shepherd Worsted from Lorna's Laces in color 58ns Magnificent Mile

C Greater Poison from The Wool Dispensary (100% superwash merino wool; 107 g; 180 yds) in color Badass Unicorn (4)

Approx 7½" long, from nose to toes

MATERIALS

Using worsted-weight yarn, (4)

A Approx 20 g (40 yds)

B Approx 5 g (10 yds)

C Approx 3 g (5 yds)

US size 5 (3.75 mm) needles

1 pair of 9 mm safety eyes

BODY

Using A, work body following instructions for Basic Biscuit Body (page 51). Add nostrils and safety eyes to CO end of unicorn before stuffing body.

Then stuff body and finish as written. When body is finished, add fringe to non-face end of body for a tail (see "Making Fringe" on page 24). I used six 12"-long pieces of C held tog, attached them to body, and trimmed to about 3"-long.

EAR

Make 2.

Rnd 1: Using A and circular needle for Magic Loop method, pick up 2 and 2 sts (see page 11) from behind and to side of eye.

Rnd 2: (K1f&b, K1) twice. (6 sts)

Rnd 3: Knit all sts.

Rnd 4: (K1f&b, K2) twice. (8 sts)

Rnds 5–7: Knit all sts.

Rnd 8: K2tog around. (4 sts)

Cut yarn and use tapestry needle to thread tail through rem sts to close ear.

HORN

Rnd 1: Using B and circular needle for Magic Loop method, pick up 3 and 3 sts between ears.

Rnds 2–11: Knit all sts.

Rnd 12: K2tog around. (3 sts)

You can add pipe cleaner to the horn as necessary to get it to stand up, but my gauge was dense enough using smaller needles to get the horn to stand up with no help.

Cut yarn and use tapestry needle to thread tail through rem sts to close horn.

Once the horn is on, add a mane in a line along the body behind the horn and ears. Using 6"-long pieces of C, I made 3 bundles of 3 strands each and attached them in 3 spots right next to each other, then trimmed the mane to about 2"-long.

LEG

Make 4.

Pick up 2 front legs on same line as ears, but on sides, and pick up 2 back legs on back rounded end by tail.

Rnd 1: Using A and circular needle for Magic Loop method, pick up 5 and 5 sts.

Rnds 2–15: Knit all sts.

Rnds 16–21: Switch to B and knit all sts. Cont in B to the end of the foot.

Rnd 22: K2tog around. (5 sts)

Stuff foot. Cut yarn and use tapestry needle to thread tail through rem sts to close foot.

Pocket-Size Phone Friend

You guessed it—this guy, knit in worsted-weight yarn, is designed to fit a smartphone, specifically one that starts with an "i." He is also great for storing other gadgets, like a digital camera. Or as wrapping for gift cards, cash, or other small treasures. Personally, I turned him into a set of Nesting Monsters as you can see on page 76 because that is what I do.

SAMPLE

A Shepherd Worsted from Lorna's Laces (100% superwash merino wool; 4 oz; 225 yds) in color Growth (4)

B Shepherd Worsted from Lorna's Laces in color Ysolda Red

C Shepherd Worsted from Lorna's Laces in color 0ns Natural

Approx 7" tall, from head to toe

MATERIALS

Using worsted-weight yarn, (4)

A Approx 16 g (32 yds)

B Approx 3 g (6 yds)

C Approx 2 g (4 yds)

US size 5 (3.75 mm) needles

2 black domed shank buttons (⅜" diameter)

BODY

Following instructions for Basic Biscuit Body (page 51), CO with A and work as follows.

Rnds 1–8: With A.

Rnds 9–25: Work in stripes of 1 rnd B, 1 rnd C, ending on a B rnd.

Rnd 26: Switch to A and knit all sts. Cont in A to end of body.

Rnd 27: BO first 16 sts of rnd, knit to end of rnd. (16 sts)

Rnd 28: Use knit CO (page 79) to CO 16 sts, then join in the round again and knit to end of rnd. (32 sts)

Rnd 29 to end of body: Work as written.

Once body is done, sew on button eyes using needle and thread. I chose to use buttons on this guy so that the ends of the safety eyes wouldn't be poking through the back and scratch my phone.

My creature's mouth was gaping open more than I wanted, so I picked up the arm stitches right next to the mouth lines to close up the mouth a bit.

LEG

Make 2.

Using A, work legs following instructions for "Basic Biscuit-Body Leg" (page 52).

ARM

Make 2.

Rnd 1: Using A and circular needle for Magic Loop method, pick up 3 sts from top rnd of shirt and 3 sts from 1 rnd below (see page 11). For both arms, be sure that beg of rnd is on underside of arm, closest to body.

Rnds 2–14: Knit all sts.

Rnd 15: K1f&b in first 3 sts, K3. (9 sts)

Rnds 16–20: Knit all sts.

Stuff hand. Cut yarn and use tapestry needle to thread tail through rem sts to close hand.

EAR

Make 2.

Rnd 1: Using A and circular needle for Magic Loop method, pick up 3 and 3 sts up the side right above arm.

Rnds 2 and 3: Knit all sts.

Rnd 4: (K1f&b, K2) twice. (8 sts)

Rnds 5 and 6: Knit all sts.

Rnd 7: (K3, K1f&b) twice. (10 sts)

Rnds 8–15: Knit all sts.

Rnd 16: K2tog around. (5 sts)

Cut yarn and use tapestry needle to thread tail through rem sts to close ear.

Basic Stitchy Body

This is definitely the biggest body in this book, and I designed it to use less than 50 yards of *two* colors, rather than one color like many of the other patterns. I knit the basic sample in one color so you could see how much yardage it would take in case you wanted to use only one color throughout.

I love this body and designed it with colorwork stitch patterns in mind. The body itself is very simple and has only one decrease round for the neck, so if you want to knit the body in a stitch pattern, you won't have to figure out how to add or subtract stitches for your pattern. You can think of the body as kind of a blank canvas, just waiting for a stitch pattern to be added.

BASIC STITCHY-BODY SAMPLE

Rios from Malabrigo (100% pure merino superwash; 100 g; 210 yds) in color 139 Pocion (4)

Approx 10" tall, from head to toe

MATERIALS

Approx 36 g (76 yds) of worsted-weight yarn in one color (4)

40" circular needle 2 or 3 sizes smaller than that recommended for your yarn (for Magic Loop method)

US size 5 (3.75 mm) needles

1 pair of 12 mm safety eyes

Pattern Note

This pattern starts out knit flat to create the base, then stitches are picked up around the base to create the body. Though it calls for a circular needle for knitting in the round, remember that knitting in the round doesn't start until after the flat base has been created.

BASIC STITCHY BODY

Using circular needle for Magic Loop method, CO 8 sts. DO NOT JOIN yet. If you prefer, use provisional CO for 8 sts here so you eliminate picking up a few sts around base.

Rows 1–24: Knit all sts (garter st).

Pick Up Stitches around Base

K8 once more. Turn corner and PU 12 sts along long edge (1 st per garter bump). Slide sts down cable to set up for working in the round using Magic Loop method. Turn corner and PU 8 sts along CO edge (or PU sts from provisional CO if applicable). Turn piece once more and PU 12 sts along final long edge (1 st per garter bump). You'll now have 40 total sts.

Begin the Body

K4, next st is first st of rnd for body. Rearrange sts on needles and PM as needed to mark new beg of rnd.

Rnds 1–22: Knit all sts.

Rnd 23: (K2tog, K2) around. (30 sts)

Rnds 24–34: Knit all sts.

Rnd 35: (Ssk, K11, K2tog) twice. (26 sts)

Rnd 36: (Ssk, K9, K2tog) twice. (22 sts)

Rnd 37: (Ssk, K7, K2tog) twice. (18 sts)

Attach safety eyes or add embroidery that needs to be tied off or secured on inside of body, then stuff body. Cut yarn leaving a long tail, and use tapestry needle to work Kitchener st to close sts.

BASIC STITCHY-BODY ARM

Make 2.

Rnd 1: Using circular needle for Magic Loop method, pick up 4 sts from neck dec rnd and 4 sts from 1 rnd below (see page 11).

Rnds 2–28: Knit all sts.

Rnd 29: K1f&b around. (16 sts)

Rnds 30–36: Knit all sts.

Rnd 37: K2tog around. (8 sts)

Stuff hand. Cut yarn and use tapestry needle to thread tail through rem sts to close hand.

BASIC STITCHY-BODY LEG

Make 2.

Rnd 1: Using circular needle for Magic Loop method, pick up 5 sts from base of body and 5 sts from bottom front edge of body. For both legs, be sure that beg of rnd is on *backside* of body.

Rnds 2–35: Knit all sts.

Working just first 5 sts of rnd and holding last 5 sts of rnd on your cable, work back and forth as follows.

Row 1: Sl 1, knit to end. Turn.

Row 2: Sl 1, purl to end. Turn.

Work rows 1 and 2 for a total of 6 rows, ending on a purl row.

Rnd 1 of foot: Turn work so you're ready to knit. PM to indicate new beg of rnd. Knit across heel sts once more. Using same needle tip, PU 3 sts from LH side of heel flap. Flip to other needle tip, knit across held instep sts and PU 3 sts from RH side of heel flap. (16 sts)

Rnd 2: K5, K2tog, K7, ssk. (14 sts)

Rnds 3–14: Knit all sts.

Rnd 15: K2tog around. (7 sts)

Stuff foot. Cut yarn and use tapestry needle to thread tail through rem sts to close foot.

basic stitchy body

Dinky Doggy

Perfect for the dog lover, this little guy is sure to be an instant best friend. Plus, this is one puppy you can feel good about giving as a gift since he makes a very easy-to-care-for pet!

SAMPLE

A Remix from Berroco (30% nylon, 27% cotton, 24% acrylic, 10% silk, 9% linen; 100 g/3.5 oz; 216 yds/200 m) in color 3903 Almond **[4]**

B Remix from Berroco in color 3990 Cocoa

Approx 8½" tall, from head to toe

MATERIALS

Using worsted-weight yarn, **[4]**

A Approx 23 g (50 yds)

B Approx 16 g (33 yds)

US size 5 (3.75 mm) needles

1 pair of 9 mm safety eyes

15 mm safety nose

EYE PATCH

Knit eye patch first so it can be sewn on before closing body. Using B and circular needle for Magic Loop method, CO 4 sts and join for working in the round, making sure not to twist sts. PM to indicate beg of rnd.

Rnd 1: K1f&b around. (8 sts)

Rnd 2: Knit all sts.

Rnd 3: K1f&b around. (16 sts)

Loosely BO all sts.

BODY

Using B and following instructions for Basic Stitchy Body (page 63), CO and work base. Switch to A, pick up sts, and work through rem of body.

ARM

Make 2.

Rnd 1: Using A and circular needle for Magic Loop method, pick up 4 sts from neck dec rnd and 4 sts from 1 rnd below (see page 11).

Rnds 2 and 3: Knit all sts.

Rnd 4: (K1f&b, K3) twice. (10 sts)

Rnds 5 and 6: Knit all sts.

Rnd 7: (K4, K1f&b) twice. (12 sts)

Rnds 8–15: Knit all sts.

Rnds 16–22: Switch to B and knit all sts.

Rnd 23: K2tog around. (6 sts)

Stuff hand. Cut yarn and use tapestry needle to thread tail through rem sts to close hand.

LEG

Make 2.

Rnd 1: Using A and circular needle for Magic Loop method, pick up 4 sts from base of body and 4 sts from bottom front edge of body.

Rnds 2 and 3: Knit all sts.

Rnd 4: (K1f&b, K3) twice. (10 sts)

Rnds 5 and 6: Knit all sts.

Rnd 7: (K4, K1f&b) twice. (12 sts)

Rnds 8–18: Knit all sts.

Rnds 19–26: Switch to B and knit all sts.

Rnd 27: K2tog around. (6 sts)

Stuff foot. Cut yarn and use tapestry needle to thread tail through rem sts to close foot.

basic stitchy body

TAIL

Rnd 1: Using A and circular needle for Magic Loop method, pick up 4 and 4 sts from bottom center of back of body.

Rnds 2–18: Knit all sts

Rnds 19–25: Switch to B and knit all sts.

Cut yarn and use tapestry needle to thread tail through rem sts to close tail.

EAR

Make 2.

Rnd 1: Using B and circular needle for Magic Loop method, pick up 4 and 4 sts from front to back on side of top of head.

Rnd 2: Knit all sts.

Rnd 3: (K1f&b, K2, K1f&b) twice. (12 sts)

Rnd 4: Knit all sts.

Rnd 5: (K1f&b, K4, K1f&b) twice. (16 sts)

Rnds 6–15: Knit all sts.

Rnd 16: (Ssk, K4, K2tog) twice. (12 sts)

Rnd 17: Knit all sts.

Rnd 18: (Ssk, K2, K2tog) twice. (8 sts)

Cut yarn and use tapestry needle to thread tail through rem sts to close ear.

Button Bigfoot and Yea-Big Yeti

Sasquatch, Bigfoot, Skookum, Yeti, whatever name you give him there seem to be sightings and reports of this elusive fellow no matter where you're from. Now you can create your own myths and adventures by making a mini version of the big legend!

SAMPLE

A Fizz from Crystal Palace Yarns (100% polyester; 50 g; 120 yds) in color 9152 Wood Grain (**4**)

B Merino 5 from Crystal Palace Yarns (100% superwash merino wool; 50 g; 110 yds) in color 5239 Dark Chocolate (**4**)

Approx 8" tall, from head to foot

MATERIALS

Using worsted-weight yarn, (**4**)

A Approx 19 g (46 yds)

B Approx 8 g (18 yds)

US size 5 (3.75 mm) needles

1 pair of 12 mm safety eyes

BODY

Using A and following instructions for Basic Stitchy Body (page 63), skip base and CO 40 sts. Work as written for rest of body.

LEG

Make 2.

Rnd 1: Using A and circular needle for Magic Loop method, from bottom edge of body, pick up 5 sts from front CO edge and 5 sts from back CO edge (see page 11). For both legs, be sure that beg of rnd is on *backside* of body.

Rnds 2–24: Knit all sts.

Rnd 25: Switch to B and knit all sts. You'll cont in B to end of foot.

Working just first 5 sts of rnd and holding last 5 sts of rnd on your cable, work as follows.

Row 1: Sl 1, knit to end. Turn.

basic stitchy body

Row 2: Sl 1, purl to end. Turn.

Work rows 1 and 2 for a total of 4 rows, ending on a purl row.

Rnd 1 of foot: Turn work so you're ready to knit. PM to indicate new beg of rnd. Knit across heel sts once more. Using same needle tip, PU 3 sts from LH side of heel flap (2 gusset sts plus 1 st in gap). Flip to other needle tip and knit across held instep sts and PU 3 sts from RH side of heel flap (2 gusset sts plus 1 st in gap). (16 sts)

Rnd 2: K5, K2tog, K7, ssk. (14 sts)

Rnds 3 and 4: Knit all sts.

Rnd 5: K4, K1f&b, knit to last st, K1f&b. (16 sts)

Rnds 6 and 7: Knit all sts.

Rnd 8: K5, K1f&b, knit to last st, K1f&b. (18 sts)

Rnds 9 and 10: Knit all sts.

Rnd 11: K6, K1f&b, knit to last st, K1f&b. (20 sts)

Rnds 12–14: Knit all sts.

Rnd 15: (Ssk, K6, K2tog) twice. (16 sts)

Continued on page 68.

Yea-Big Yeti

This Yeti was knit using the same pattern as the Button Bigfoot. The only difference is I knit the base for the Yeti with B (the base was left out for the Bigfoot). While these two critters were knit using the same pattern and same size needles, the Yeti is much bigger than the Bigfoot because the Splash yarn used to create the Yeti is a much bulkier yarn than the Fizz used for the Bigfoot.

SAMPLE

A Splash from Crystal Palace Yarns (100% polyester; 100 g; 85 yds) in color 7192 Italian Ice (**5**)

B Merino 5 from Crystal Palace Yarns (100% superwash merino wool; 50 g; 110 yds) in color 5204 Natural Ecru (**4**)

Approx 13" tall, from head to toe

MATERIALS

A Approx 51 g (44 yds) of bulky-weight novelty yarn (**5**)

B Approx 13 g (29 yds) of worsted-weight yarn (**4**)

US size 5 (3.75 mm) needles

1 pair of 12 mm safety eyes

Follow the instructions for Button Bigfoot and Yea-Big Yeti (page 66), except work the 24-row base of the Basic Stitchy Body (page 63) using B.

Continued from Button Bigfoot on page 67.

Stuff foot. Cut yarn, leaving a long tail, and use tapestry needle to work Kitchener st across sts.

Once you're done with legs, add eyes and mouth, stuff body, and then whipstitch base closed between legs.

ARM

Make 2.

Rnd 1: Using A and circular needle for Magic Loop method, pick up 5 sts from neck dec rnd and 5 sts from 1 rnd below.

Rnds 2–24: Knit all sts.

Rnds 25–32: Switch to B and knit all sts.

Stuff hand. Cut yarn and use tapestry needle to thread tail through rem sts to close hand.

Olive-Sized Owl

This guy, with his zigzaggy tummy, is a fun take on the creature that seems to be everywhere. Make a couple of these guys in nursery colors for perfect baby decor, or decorate a fun woodland-creatures-themed table to be the high-light of your next kids' party!

SAMPLE

A Superwash Worsted from SweetGeorgia Yarns (100% super-wash merino wool; 115 g; 200 yds) in color Pistachio (4)

B Superwash Worsted from SweetGeorgia Yarns in color Bison

Approx 7" tall, from head to base

MATERIALS

Using worsted-weight yarn, (4)

A Approx 29 g (50 yds)

B Approx 9 g (16 yds)

US size 5 (3.7 5 mm) needles

1 pair of 15 mm safety eyes

Scrap of yellow yarn for beak

BODY

Using A and following instructions for Basic Stitchy Body (page 63), CO and work base for 28 rows rather than 24 rows.

Rnd 1: Switch to B to work PU rnd of body as follows: PU 8 sts on ends as written, but PU 14 sts per long side rather than 12. Body will be 44 sts around.

For rnds 2–24 of body, work in zigzag patt and stripes of 2 rnds B, 2 rnds A, ending on a B stripe on rnd 24.

Rnd 2 and all even-numbered rnds: (K1f&b, K3, DD, K3, K1f&b) 4 times. (44 sts)

Rnd 3: Knit all sts.

Rnds 4–22: Rep rnds 2 and 3, ending with rnd 2.

Rnd 23: Switch to A, (K2tog, K2) around (33 sts). You'll cont in A to end of body.

Rnd 24: K2tog, K31. (32 sts)

Rnds 25–36: Knit all sts.

Stop and attach safety eyes, and embroider yellow V for a beak.

Rnd 37: K5, and place these 5 sts plus last 5 sts of rnd on waste yarn. Work Kitchener st over next 6 and last 6 sts of rnd. You'll have 10 sts left on your needle, and 10 sts left on your waste yarn. Stuff body now while you still have easy access.

HORN

Make 2.

First Horn

Rnd 1: Join yarn (to beg knitting again) and knit 10 sts left on your needle. At end of rnd, work across gap to rejoin for working in the round.

Rnd 2: Knit all sts.

Rnd 3: (Ssk, K3) twice. (8 sts)

Rnd 4: Knit all sts.

Rnd 5: (K2, K2tog) twice. (6 sts)
Add any last bits of stuffing now. Cut yarn and use tapestry needle to thread tail through rem sts to close horn.

Second Horn

Move rem 10 sts from waste yarn to your needles, work as for first horn.

WING

Make 2.

Rnd 1: Using A and circular needle for Magic Loop method, pick up 7 sts from neck dec rnd and 7 sts from 1 rnd below (see page 11).

Rnd 2: (K1f&b, K5, K1f&b) twice. (18 sts)

Rnds 3–16: Knit all sts.

Rnd 17: (Ssk, K7) twice. (16 sts)

Rnds 18 and 19: Knit all sts.

Rnd 20: (K6, K2tog) twice. (14 sts)

Rnds 21 and 22: Knit all sts.

Rnd 23: (Ssk, K3, K2tog) twice. (10 sts)

Rnd 24: (Ssk, K1, K2tog) twice. (6 sts)

Cut yarn and use tapestry needle to thread tail through rem sts to close wing.

Weensy Woodland Friend

Bunny? Rodent? Whatever you think this guy looks like, you have to agree that he is super cute. I wanted to feature this cool stitch pattern as a nice little shirt for this guy. Add arms if you want; I thought he looked perfect without them!

basic stitchy body

A   Rios from Malabrigo (100% pure merino superwash; 100 g; 210 yds) in color 43 Plomo (4)

B   Rios from Malabrigo in color 611 Ravelry Red

C   Rios from Malabrigo in color 63 Natural

Approx 8½" tall, from ears to toes

MATERIALS

Using worsted-weight yarn, (4)

A   Approx 12 g (26 yds)

B   Approx 6 g (13 yds)

C   Approx 5 g (11 yds)

US size 5 (3.75 mm) needles

1 pair of 9 mm safety eyes

STITCH PATTERN

Rnd 1: With C, (K1, sl 1) to end.

Rnd 2: With C, knit all sts.

Rnd 3: With B, K2, (sl 1, K1) to end.

Rnd 4: With B, knit all sts.

Rep rnds 1–4 for patt.

BODY

Following instructions for Basic Stitchy Body (page 63), work body without base as follows.

Using B and circular needle for Magic Loop method, CO 40 sts and join for working in the round, making sure not to twist sts. PM to indicate beg of rnd.

Sl all sts purlwise wyib.

Rnd 1: Knit all sts.

Rnds 2–29: Work 7 reps of st patt.

Rnd 30: Switch to A, (K2tog, K2) around. (30 sts). Cont in A to end of body.

Rnds 31–38: Knit all sts.

Rnd 39: (Ssk, K11, K2tog) twice. (26 sts)

Rnd 40: (Ssk, K9, K2tog) twice. (22 sts)

Rnd 41: (Ssk, K7, K2tog) twice. (18 sts)

Cut yarn leaving a long tail, and use tapestry needle to work Kitchener st across top of head to close sts.

LEG

Make 2.

Rnd 1: Using A and circular needle for Magic Loop method, from CO edge of body, pick up 5 sts from front CO edge and 5 sts from back CO edge (see page 11).

Rnds 2 and 3: Knit all sts.

Rnd 4: (K1f&b, K4) twice. (12 sts)

Rnds 5 and 6: Knit all sts.

Rnd 7: (K5, K1f&b) twice. (14 sts)

Rnds 8–24: Knit all sts.

Rnd 25: K2tog around. (7 sts)

Stuff leg. Cut yarn and use tapestry needle to thread tail through rem sts to close leg. Attach eyes and embroider nose, then stuff body and whipstitch base closed between legs.

EAR

Make 2.

Rnd 1: Using A and circular needle for Magic Loop method, pick up 3 and 3 sts from one side of top of head.

Rnd 2: Knit all sts.

Rnd 3: (K1, K1f&b, K1) twice. (8 sts)

Rnds 4–9: Knit all sts.

Cut yarn and use tapestry needle to thread tail through rem sts to close ear.

Slight Swimmer

Here's a tiny old-time swimmer, complete with inner-tube. Awesome-sauce, right? This book includes my first knitted people patterns, and I have to say, after this guy, I am hooked and want to create more tiny knitted people!

SAMPLE

Shepherd Worsted from Lorna's Laces (100% superwash merino wool; 4 oz; 225 yds) (4) in the following colors:

A color 16ns Charcoal

B color 0ns Natural

C color 15ns Chino

D color 54ns Firefly

Approx 10" tall, from head to toe

MATERIALS

Using worsted-weight yarn, (4)

A Approx 8 g (17 yds)

B Approx 7 g (15 yds)

C Approx 20 g (42 yds)

D Approx 8 g (17 yds)

US size 5 (3.75 mm) needles

1 pair of 12 mm safety eyes

Notions: extra circular needle in same size as your main circular needle (any length), waste yarn for provisional cast on

BODY

Using A and following instructions for Basic Stitchy Body (page 63), CO and work 24-rnd base as written.

Switch to B for PU rnd and work body as follows.

Rnds 1–18: Work in stripes of 2 rnds B, 2 rnds A.

Rnds 19–20: K4 in A, K12 in C, K8 in A, K12 in C, K4 in A.

Rnds 21 and 22: K4 in B, K12 in C, K8 in B, K12 in C, K4 in B.

Rnd 23: Switch to C (K2tog, K2) around (30 sts). You'll remain in C to end of body.

Rnd 24 to end of body: Work as written.

When the body is finished, cut 7 pieces of black yarn 6" long, and make fringe across the top of the head for hair (see "Making Fringe" on page 24). Starting in the middle, put fringe on 7 spots for the hair. Once you're happy with the hair placement, trim the fringe very short (½" or shorter). If desired, add 3 spots of fringe for chest hair. Leave out the chest hair if your swimmer is a girl!

ARM

Make 2.

Rnd 1: Using C and circular needle for Magic Loop method, pick up 5 sts from rnd 22 of body and 5 sts from 1 rnd below (see page 11).

Rnds 2–24: Knit all sts.

Rnd 25: (K1f&b, K3, K1f&b) twice. (14 sts)

Rnds 26–34: Knit all sts.

Rnd 35: (Ssk, K3, K2tog) twice. (10 sts)

Stuff hand. Cut yarn leaving a long tail and use tapestry needle to work Kitchener st to close rem sts.

LEG

Make 2.

Rnd 1: Using B and circular needle for Magic Loop method, pick up 5 sts from base of body and 5 sts from bottom front edge of body. For both legs, be sure that beg of rnd is on *backside* of body.

Rnds 2–12: Knit all sts working in stripes of 2 rnds B, 2 rnds A.

Rnds 13–28: Switch to C and knit all sts. Cont in C to end of foot.

Working just first 5 sts of rnd and holding last 5 sts of rnd on cable, work back and forth as follows.

Row 1: Sl 1, knit to end. Turn.

Row 2: Sl 1, purl to end. Turn.

Work rows 1 and 2 for a total of 4 rows, ending on a purl row.

Rnd 1 of foot: Turn your work so you're ready to knit. PM to indicate new beg of rnd. Knit across heel sts once more. Using same needle tip, PU 3 sts from LH side of heel flap (2 gusset sts plus 1 st in gap). Flip to other needle tip and knit across held instep sts and PU 3 sts from RH side of heel flap (2 gusset sts plus 1 st in gap). (16 sts)

Rnd 2: Knit all sts.

Rnd 3: K4, K2tog, K2tog, K4, ssk, ssk. (12 sts)

Rnds 4 and 5: Knit all sts.

Rnd 6: (K5, K1f&b) twice. (14 sts)

Rnds 7 and 8: Knit all sts.

Rnd 9: (K1f&b, K6) twice. (16 sts)

Rnds 10–12: Knit all sts.

Rnd 13: (Ssk, K4, K2tog) twice. (12 sts)

Stuff foot. Cut yarn, leaving a long tail, and work Kitchener st to close sts.

INNER TUBE

With D, your circular needle, and waste yarn, use provisional CO to CO 36 sts. DO NOT JOIN.

Knit 1 row.

Slide half the sts to each needle tip to set up for working in the round using Magic Loop method. Join sts to beg working in the round by cont to knit from last st you just knit to first st you knit after CO.

Rnds 1–17: Knit all sts.

Now you're ready to bind off. Slip the provisional CO sts to a second circular needle and remove the waste yarn.

Move that needle up through center of project, so it's right next to needle you have been working on. This will fold your piece and place the first and last rnds next to each other, essentially "halfing" the length of your piece.

Cut working yarn, leaving a tail that's about 4 times the project's circumference. With your tapestry needle work Kitchener st, moving from beg of rnd just completed to provisional CO sts.

Note: The provisional CO will leave every other stitch twisted, so untwist them as you come to them. Cont Kitchener st around ring, stopping every couple of inches to stuff ring. If you end up a st short at end, just pick 1 up.

Weave in ends and twist grafted seam to inside of ring.

basic stitchy body

Puny Pocket Playmate

When I started this book, I wanted to be sure to include a couple of patterns that had pockets or pouches like this guy and Pocket-Size Phone Friend on page 60, which are perfect for a gift card or cash. I know a lot of knitters who like to give a little knitted critter as a gift. Why not tuck a little something extra in his pocket? This little fella is my absolute favorite! I love everything about him, but those giant ears and eyes just kill me!

SAMPLE

A Shepherd Worsted from Lorna's Laces (100% superwash merino wool; 4 oz; 225 yds) in Patina (4)

B Shepherd Worsted from Lorna's Laces in color 211 Monkeyshines

Approx 10" tall, from head to toe

MATERIALS

Using worsted-weight yarn, (4)

A Approx 28 g (56 yds)

B Approx 11 g (22 yds)

Scrap of black yarn for face

US size 5 (3.75 mm) needles

1 pair of 15 mm safety eyes

BODY

Using B, follow instructions for Basic Stitchy Body (page 63) to CO and work base and body through rnd 22.

Rnds 23 to end of body: Switch to A and work as written.

Add eyes before stuffing and closing body. Once body is finished, embroider nose and mouth using a scrap of black yarn.

POCKET

Pocket is knit flat (not in the round).

Row 1: Using any needle and A, PU 12 sts in a straight line along front edge of body, where base meets body.

Rows 2–18: Starting with a purl row, work all sts in St st (knit on RS, purl on WS).

Rows 19 and 20: (K1, P1) across.

Loosely BO all sts in patt.

ARM

Make 2.

Using A, work arms following instructions for "Basic Stitchy Body Arm" (page 64).

LEG

Make 2.

Using A, work legs following instructions for "Basic Stitchy-Body Leg" (page 64).

EAR

Make 2.

Rnd 1: Using A and circular needle for Magic Loop method, starting near top of head and working downward, pick up 7 sts from side of head, then slide those sts down the cable to other needle tip and pick up 7 from bottom to top (see page 11). Be sure that beg of rnd starts at top of head.

Rnd 2: (K1f&b, K5, K1f&b) twice. (18 sts)

Rnds 3–7: Knit all sts.

Rnd 8: K2tog around. (9 sts)

Cut yarn and use tapestry needle to thread tail through rem sts to close ear.

Beyond the Basics: What to Do With Your Little Knits

So you may be thinking to yourself, "Sure, these little knits are fun and all, and a great way to use up all of my scrap and handspun yarns, but what the heck am I going to do with all of my tiny creations?" In the next few pages, I hope to give you a bunch of ideas to get your creative juices flowing!

ALL DECKED OUT

These little knits are absolutely perfect for holiday decorations! Bats, ghosts, and candy-corn creatures displayed on a Halloween table (shown on page 75) is just one idea of how to use your creations for holidays. Simply switch out colors in sweaters or bodies for other holidays—red, green, and white for Christmas; pink and red for Valentine's Day; pastels for Easter. Think of how cute an all-green table would be for St. Paddy's Day! Or what about red, white, and blue critters to celebrate Independence Day? Get in the holiday spirit, get creative, and get knitting!

Bats

Use the instructions for Itty-Bitty Batty (page 25). For the medium bat, refer to the materials list in the pattern; for the large bat, use approximately 126 yards of worsted-weight yarn (Rios from Malabrigo) and work with two strands of yarn held together on size 9 needles. The large bat stands about 6" tall and has 18 mm safety eyes.

Ghosts

Use the Basic Stitchy Body (page 63) with no arms or legs. You'll need the following for each of the ghosts.

Small ghost: Approximately 24 yards of white sock yarn (Heritage Sock Yarn from Cascade Yarns) and size 1 needles. Ghost is about 3½" tall and has 9 mm safety eyes.

Medium ghost: Approximately 60 yards of the same sock yarn as the small ghost and work with two strands of yarn held together on size 4 needles. Ghost is about 5" tall and has 12 mm safety eyes.

Large ghost: Approximately 106 yards of white worsted-weight yarn (220 Superwash from Cascade Yarns) and work with two strands of yarn held together on size 9 needles. Ghost is about 8" tall and has 18 mm safety eyes.

Pumpkin Monster

Use the Basic Uni-Body (page 41) and approximately 40 yards of pumpkin worsted-weight yarn (220 Superwash from Cascade Yarns) worked on size 5 needles. Pumpkin is about 5" tall and has an embroidered face.

Candy-Corn Creatures

Use the Basic Stitchy Body (page 63) and sock yarn (Heritage Sock Yarn from Cascade Yarns).

Small candy corn: Approximately 36 yards of lemon and 2 to 4 yards each of pumpkin and white on size 1 needles. Corn is about 6½" from top to toe and has 9 mm safety eyes.

Large candy corn: Approximately 96 yards of lemon and 20 yards each of pumpkin and white and work with two strands of yarn held together on size 4 needles. Corn is about 10" from top to toe and has 15 mm safety eyes.

BAT MOBILE

For this mobile, cover the inside of an embroidery hoop in ribbon using sparkle Mod Podge and hang it with ribbon. Add five Itty-Bitty Batty creatures (page 25) knit in sock yarn and hang them with ribbon from the back of their bodies to make it look like they're in flight. Isn't this the perfect decoration to take this Halloween table up another notch to amazing? Not just for holiday decorations, this mobile would be darling above a crib as well, as long as you have a love for Morticia Addams like I do. (She was a knitter, you know!) If bats aren't your idea of baby-friendly creatures, why not make this mobile and attach elephants, monkeys, or unicorns instead?

Follow instructions for Itty-Bitty Batty. For each bat, you'll need approximately 35 yards of black sock yarn (Heritage Sock Yarn from Cascade Yarns) and size 1 needles. Bat is about 3" tall and has 9 mm safety eyes.

GIANT-IZE YOUR LITTLES

I know this book is supposed to be all little knits, but as I was knitting all of the samples, I couldn't help but think about bulky yarns and holding multiple strands of yarns together to supersize my small creatures. The Nano Ninja (page 43) looks awesome huge! I made one for my son, and he is always sneaking his way around the house and popping out when least expected (like ninjas tend to do!).

Follow instructions for Nano Ninja and use three strands of yarn held together on size 13 needles. I used Shepherd Worsted from Lorna's Laces in the following amounts and colors:

A Approximately 255 yards in color 58ns Kerfuffle

B Approximately 7 yards in color
0ns Natural

Giant Ninja is about 11" tall and
has 18 mm safety eyes.

MONSTER MATRYOSHKA

I loved how my Pocket-Size Phone Friend (page 60) turned out, and I knew immediately he would be excellent for all sorts of things other than holding my phone. The first thing that came to mind was how adorable it would be to do a whole family of monsters to nest inside each other. How cute would it be to give this as a gift with money or a gift card or a small treasure hiding inside the smallest monster?

Follow the instructions for Pocket-Size Phone Friend. I used Shepherd Sock Sport, Worsted, and Bulky yarns and black domed shank buttons for the eyes. You'll need the following amounts and needles for each of the monsters.

Tiny (4½") monster: Approximately 39 yards of sock yarn, size 1 needle, and ⅛"-diameter buttons.

Small (5½") monster: Approximately 46 yards of sock yarn, size 3 needles, and ¼"-diameter buttons.

Medium (7") monster: Approximately 48 yards of worsted-weight yarn, size 5 needles, and ⅜"-diameter buttons.

Large (9") monster: Approximately 64 yards of bulky-weight yarn, size 9 needles, and ⅝"-diameter buttons.

EGG-CELLENT!

Think of how cute it would be to create an egg cozy! Just leave the bottom open and the base off from the Basic Bowling-Pin Body (page 29) or the Basic Stitchy Body (page 63), or omit the legs from the Basic Uni-Body (page 41). Need a cute way to display your little knits? Sit them on an eggcup on a shelf!

Follow instructions for Bantam Bunny (page 38), but do not knit the legs, stuff the body, or sew the bottom shut for this guy. I used size 1 needles and Heritage Sock Yarn from Cascade Yarns in the following amounts and colors:

A Approximately 31 yards in color 5618 Snow

B Approximately 9 yards in color 5630 Annis

C Approximately 9 yards in color 5644 Lemon

Bunny is about 4" tall and has 6 mm safety eyes and a 9 mm safety nose.

TAG, YOU'RE IT!

Sometimes it's fun to make a little something extra to make a special gift that much more extraordinary. I made a cute ornament to top a present by knitting this little elephant. Hanging from a gift bag, he makes this gift extra cute!

beyond the basics: what to do with your little knits

Follow insructions for Small-Peanuts Elephant (page 32), using red and green in one round per color stripes for the sweater instead of the one color called for. I used size 1 needles and Heritage Sock Yarn from Cascade Yarns in the following amounts and colors:

A   Approximately 35 yards in color 5660 Grey

B   Approximately 9 yards in color 5659 Primavera

C   Approximately 9 yards in color 5661 Zinnia Red

Elephant is about 5" tall and has 6 mm safety eyes.

SHAKE IT UP

All of these little knits are perfectly sized for baby hands! My son was about 12 to18 months old as I was writing and finishing everything for this book. He would be completely uninterested in whatever I was knitting until I added the eyes. As soon as he saw the eyes, he'd want to hug my project. Seeing him do this made me realize that dropping a rattle in any of these projects would make them awesome for little ones. Embroider the eyes if you're giving the toy to someone under the age of three. I picked the Weensy Woodland Friend (page 69) since its lack of arms would make it easy for little hands to grab. Hey, little knits for little ones! Who'd-a-thunk it?

Follow instructions for Weensy Woodland Friend, using two strands of worsted-weight yarn held together and size 9 needles. I used Rios from Malabrigo in the following amounts and colors:

A   Approximately 74 yards in color 43 Plomo

B   Approximately 36 yards in color 96 Sunset

C   Approximately 32 yards in color 63 Natural

Critter is about 12" tall and has 18 mm safety eyes. You'll need one small rattle insert. See "Where to Get the Goods" on page 79.

GET CREATIVE

Think outside the box and take any of these patterns another step further! I turned the bowling ball from Mini Monster Bowling (page 34) into a Tribble—perfect for any Star Trek fan—by knitting it in eyelash yarn. All of these patterns could become a million different things with just a little imagination.

Follow instructions for the bowling ball in Mini Monster Bowling (page 35). You'll need approximately 27 yards of eyelash yarn (Splash from Crystal Palace Yarns) and size 5 needles. Tribble is about 6" tall and has 18 mm safety eyes.

Useful Information

STANDARD YARN-WEIGHT SYSTEM						
Yarn-Weight Symbol and Category Name	**1** Super Fine	**2** Fine	**3** Light	**4** Medium	**5** Bulky	**6** Super Bulky
Types of Yarn in Category	Sock, Fingering, Baby	Sport, Baby	DK, Light Worsted	Worsted, Afghan, Aran	Chunky, Craft, Rug	Bulky, Roving
Knit Gauge Range* in Stockinette Stitch to 4"	27 to 32 sts	23 to 26 sts	21 to 24 sts	16 to 20 sts	12 to 15 sts	6 to 11 sts
Recommended Needle in Metric Size Range	2.25 to 3.25 mm	3.25 to 3.75 mm	3.75 to 4.5 mm	4.5 to 5.5 mm	5.5 to 8 mm	8 mm and larger
Recommended Needle in US Size Range	1 to 3	3 to 5	5 to 7	7 to 9	9 to 11	11 and larger

These are guidelines only. The above reflect the most commonly used gauges and needles for specific yarn categories.

METRIC CONVERSIONS

Yards x .91 = meters
Meters x 1.09 = yards
Ounces x 28.35 = grams
Grams x .035 = ounces

Abbreviations and Glossary

( ) Work instructions within parentheses as many times as directed

approx approximately

beg begin(ning)

BO bind off

CO cast on

cont continue(ing)(s)

DD double decrease: slip 2 stitches together knitwise, knit 1 stitch, pass the 2 slipped stitches over the knit stitch—2 stitches decreased

dec(s) decrease(ing)(s)

dpn(s) double-pointed needle(s)

I-cord Using two double-pointed needles, cast on specified number of stitches; usually 3 or 4. *Knit the stitches, do NOT turn, slide stitches to other end of needle. Pulling yarn firmly across the back, repeat from * until cord is required length.

inc(s) increase(ing)(s)

join begin to knit in the round

K knit

K1f&b Knit into front and back of same stitch—1 stitch increased

K2tog knit 2 stitches together—1 stitch decreased

knit CO Knit cast on: With stitches on left needle, knit the first stitch but leave stitch on the left needle, rotate right needle clockwise and insert tip of left needle into the stitch from left to right and remove from right needle—1 stitch added to left needle. Repeat as needed.

LH left hand

mm millimeter(s)

oz ounce(s)

P purl

P2tog purl 2 stitches together—1 stitch decreased

patt(s) pattern(s)

pick up slide needle through required number of stitches (see page 11)

PM place marker

PU Pick up and knit: Insert right needle into stitch and pull working yarn through stitch and onto right needle—1 stitch picked up. Repeat as needed.

rem remain(ing)

rep(s) repeat(s)

RH right hand

rnd(s) round(s)

RS right side

sl slip

sl 1 slip 1 stitch purlwise unless otherwise indicated

sl1-K2tog-psso slip 1 stitch knitwise, knit 2 stitches together, pass slipped stitch over the knit 2 together—2 sts decreased

ssk slip 2 stitches knitwise, one at a time, to right needle, then insert left needle from left to right into front loops and knit 2 stitches together—1 stitch decreased

st(s) stitch(es)

St st(s) stockinette stitch(es)

tog together

WS wrong side

wyib with yarn in back

yd(s) yard(s)

Where to Get the Goods

Contact the following yarn companies to find shops in your area that carry the yarns featured in this book.

Another Crafty Girl
www.anothercraftygirl.com
Merino Worsted

Berroco
www.berroco.com
Remix

Cascade Yarns
www.cascadeyarns.com
128 Superwash, 220 Superwash, 220 Superwash Sport, Heritage 150 Sock Yarn, Heritage Sock Yarn, Magnum

Crystal Palace Yarns
www.straw.com
Fizz, Merino 5, Splash

Lorna's Laces
www.lornaslaces.net
Shepherd Bulky, Shepherd Sock, Shepherd Sport, Shepherd Worsted

Malabrigo
www.malabrigoyarn.com
Rios

SweetGeorgia Yarns
www.sweetgeorgiayarns.com
Superwash Worsted

The Wool Dispensary
www.thewooldispensary.com
Greater Poison

Safety eyes, buttons, and embroidery hoops can be found at most major craft stores, or many places online.

Rattle inserts can be found many places online. I found mine on etsy.com by searching for "rattle inserts."

Acknowledgments

A huge thank-you to everyone for making this book possible. I love writing, and it is such a big thrill that I am able to write my third book.

- To the folks at Martingale, thank you for believing in yet another of my wacky ideas. You guys are the best.

- To my agent Linda, thank you again for being so amazing.

- To Mr. Danger and Master Danger, you guys sure are an awesome family!

- To my mother-in-law, Jen, thank you so much for your help in the eleventh hour(s)!

- To my family, thanks for the continued support and encouragement.

- Thank you again to all of the yarn companies for so generously donating the yarn in this book. In particular, thank you to Lorna's Laces for dying up all of the amazing mini-skeins!

- And to my fabulous customers, thanks for continuing to support my monster, and now little-knit mania!

About the Author

Rebecca Danger is a knitting pattern designer who lives in a fun 1950's rambler in Bothell, Washington, with her husband, Mr. Danger; their son, Presley; their two pugs, Abbey and Lucy; and a whole menagerie of knitted toys. She's got a great blog at RebeccaDanger.typepad.com and a monster of a website at DangerCrafts.com.

Rebecca believes that knitting is a lifestyle, not just a hobby. She started knitting rather obsessively and writing patterns of her original toy designs in February 2009. She really likes this lifestyle, since it means she gets to knit all day, tell the government that all of her yarn purchases are business expenses, and still be able to afford to feed her family. She also feels quite proud that all of that knitting in high school and college has lead to something more than just frowns and disgruntled looks from teachers.

What's your creative passion?

Find it at **ShopMartingale.com**

books • eBooks • ePatterns • daily blog • free projects
videos • tutorials • inspiration • giveaways

Martingale®
Create with Confidence

80